LISTEN TO YOUR FOOTSTEPS
Reflections & Essays

Kojo Baffoe

MACMILLAN

First published in 2021
by Pan Macmillan South Africa
Private Bag X19
Northlands
2116
Johannesburg
South Africa

www.panmacmillan.co.za

ISBN 978-1-77010-780-9
E-ISBN 978-1-77010-781-6

© Kojo Baffoe 2021

All rights reserved. No part of this publication may be reproduced, stored in or introduced into a retrieval system, or transmitted, in any form, or by any means (electronic, mechanical, photocopying, recording or otherwise), without the prior written permission of the publisher. Any person who does any unauthorised act in relation to this publication may be liable to criminal prosecution and civil claims for damages.

Editing by Sally Hines
Proofreading by Sean Fraser
Design and typesetting by Nyx Design
Cover design by K4
Front cover photograph by Victor Dlamini

'Those who know Kojo would have known what to expect in Listen to Your Footsteps: a deeply personal, authentic and equally intellectual journey of a quintessential African. A storyteller for the ages, every word and anecdote is like being alone with him in a quiet place as he narrates what it takes to be a real man, doting father, loving son, devoted friend and committed partner. Equally at ease in front of and behind a camera and microphone, or reading or writing, I expected him to be able to weave a story. But this was more than a story. It was a tome of a real African life – of love, loss and lessons. His anecdotes of the loss and longing for his mother, the relationship with his father, of his struggles and triumphs as a son, father and husband, of being a man, draw you into a reflection of your own standing and stance in a world that has unresolved issues with what it means to be a man. More than anything, Listen to Your Footsteps is a love story and history lesson. His story. Our story. An elegant and authentic reminder of who we are as a people, Africans and humans, by one of our finest storytellers.'
– THEBE IKALAFENG, founder and principal at Africa Brand Leadership Academy

'An insightful memoir of Kojo growing up, navigating family and figuring out his contribution to the world that reads as a beautiful ode to his father. With every word he writes there is a sense of responsibility to leave the world better than he found it. A true wordsmith; the landscape of his memories dances on the page.'
– TUMI MORAKE, comedian and author of And then Mama Said

'"I have lived a thousand lives ..." writes Kojo and Listen To Your Footsteps lets you, albeit almost too briefly, in to his youth in Maseru, his struggles with addiction and melancholy, the immense losses that have shaped him into the African man and father he is today, and his relationship with the world around him. The questions Kojo will almost never get answers to – trying to make sense of his identity; his mistakes and achievements; his parenting style; and being under the omnipresent guidance of his father – are laid candidly bare in this absorbing recollection of his life.'
– MELANIE BALA, broadcaster, Metro FM

To my mother and father, Elfi and Frank Baffoe
And to Estelle, Kweku and Ayanna,
All of whom make me want to be the best version of myself.

'I am not African because I was born in Africa but because Africa was born in me.'
– KWAME NKRUMAH

'Making the decision to have a child – it is momentous. It is to decide forever to have your heart go walking around outside your body.'
– ELIZABETH STONE

'The best way of training the young is to train yourself at the same time; not to admonish them, but to be seen never doing that of which you would admonish them.'
– PLATO

'He who has a *why* to live can bear almost any *how*.'
– FRIEDRICH NIETZSCHE

'The happiness of your life depends upon the quality of your thoughts: therefore, guard accordingly, and take care that you entertain no notions unsuitable to virtue and reasonable nature.'
– MARCUS AURELIUS

Contents

A story   1

LIKE FATHER, LIKE SON   7
MOTHER   59
GROWING UP   75
IDENTITY AND BELONGING   113
CREATIVITY   147
BEING THERE   189
BEING IN THE WORLD   237

Acknowledgements   295

A story

THESE ARE stories. My stories. Well, most of them. Some of them may be memories of stories that do not belong to me. A friend once said to me that I have a story for everything. I wanted to tell him, 'No, I don't', but then a story came to mind. And I told him that story. I can't remember that story, but perhaps it will rear its confusing head somewhere in these pages.

I have been writing words for most of my life. Some of them have been good, usually at the time of writing. Many haven't, at least when I read over them. The one guarantee is that when enough time has passed between the writing and the reading, I find my writing cringeworthy. I try not to reread my own writing once it has been put out into the world.

My father – you'll hear me say that a lot – said that when you want to make sense of things, take them out of your head and put them on the page, so I have tried to do this, often. Sometimes, when I am lucky, they have made sense on the page, as they shifted and morphed, or is it as I shifted and morphed?

In the early days, I would sit at the old Amstrad computer – young ones, Google it – in his offices of Baffoe & Associates (Pty) Ltd, while waiting to be dropped off at home after school, and let the words flow, out of my head and onto the blank page on the screen. When it was time to go, I would simply switch off the computer, without saving the file – floppy disks weren't cheap. My words would float out into whatever ether there was, never to be seen again, until the next time I sat and typed thought without thought.

Eventually, I went old school when it wasn't old school and wrote on the pages of actual notebooks. I went from long, drawn-out sentences –

which I seemed to have returned to in recent years – to shorter sentences, and somewhere along the line they became poems. I reckon every writer has quirks that irritate them about themselves and their writing. Mine is being long-winded with my sentences.

My foray into writing poetry and the role that poetry played in my later life has always been painfully ironic because my relationship with poetry in high school was often rocky. Trying to remember what the teacher said the poet meant by each line, each metaphor, each image, never quite gelled with me, or maybe it was because I never seemed to get out of the poems what was intended. I would be told that the poem was about heartbreak and yet I found it comedic, or satiric, or romantic.

School does have a way of taking the joy out of most things. I studied Shakespeare's *Macbeth* for four years in a row and dabbled in some of his other plays, reluctantly. Once out of school, I read the complete works of Shakespeare while fulfilling my duties as a Rotary Exchange Student in Oldenburg, Germany. I still have the collection on my bookshelf. One day I will read them again. Although, getting into the language is another journey in itself. Like Chaucer's *Canterbury Tales* but not as cumbersome.

Anyway, I have been writing my whole life. Sometimes I have even been paid for it. Sometimes I have been praised for it. But I have never written a book. I have written poems, articles, blog posts, tweets, Facebook posts and long captions on Instagram, but I have never written an actual book.

Yes, I did publish two collections of poetry – in 2004 and 2005 – but, even with those, it has never felt like I have written a proper – whatever that means – book.

When I was heavily involved in Johannesburg's poetry scene, including running shows, my father asked me why I hadn't published a poetry collection. The primary obstacle was funds, as there were no publishers interested in publishing poetry, especially my poetry. He offered to pay for the publishing of what was released as *Voices in My Head*.

Everything was bootstrapped. I typed, edited and laid out the basics. Quick confession. It's probably better to have someone else edit your writing; there are errors in *Voices*. A friend shot the cover in the bathroom of the apartment Estelle and I were living in. It is a picture of our faces with fabric stretched over them. We invited some friends and family over to feature on the cover, their payment being supper and wine.

I found a printer, who was happy to print as long as I gave him cash. I found details for the National Library of South Africa and secured an ISBN number for the book. I printed 500 copies, which I sold primarily at open-mic nights. I was consulting at the South African Post Office around the time the book came out, so I published a second, smaller collection called *And They Say: Black Men Don't Write Love Poetry*. The intention was to put out a single-themed collection every quarter under the Backpocket Poetry Series umbrella. Short, small enough to fit in your back pocket and filled with poems on love, I paid for the printing myself. Another 500 copies. I was also able to self-fund the book launch, at which my father was the guest of honour.

Poetry has never been a best-selling genre. Most poets have other jobs, particularly in my lifetime, and I realised that, unless they knew me, people wouldn't walk into a bookshop, see my collection and part with their hard-earned cash. I gave away as many copies as I sold and sold more coming off a poetry stage than at any other time.

I have written lots of words. I have worked for magazines where I wrote five to ten thousand words regularly, usually on a monthly basis. I had a column, which ran for two to three years, called 'From the Mind's Eye' in my family's newspaper, *Southern Star*, where I ranted, raved and generally spoke on things that I was by no means an expert on but felt the need to speak on anyway. I toured the UK in 2006 for two weeks as a poet and wrote blog posts every day on MySpace.

I started an email newsletter called *Ramblings*, where, every week, I rambled on about poetry, books and life to the hundred or so subscribers I had. I started two blogs, 'Infinite Pursuit' and 'Perfect Poetry', on Blogspot, and wrote on them relatively regularly, until I didn't. They are still out there, in my digital graveyard. When I discovered Twitter in 2008, I spent the first two years in a frenetic haze, sacrificing peace of mind and family time to tweet more than 100 000 times before I came to my senses. One hundred thousand tweets at an average of 100 characters is 10 000 000 characters, which makes it a crapload of words. That's a whole book.

Yet, still no book. As so many people around me constantly remind me.

Would it be safe to say I am writing this reluctantly? All the books say that when you write a book, you should know why you are doing it. There should be a purpose. An intention. A vision. Does getting people off my back qualify as an adequate enough reason? I guess you will be the judge.

These are stories. My stories. This may be the first book I have written, but it is the fifth book I have started to write. The first was actually 'The Prince and I', a book about fatherhood and the lessons I was learning about life from my son. I wrote about 15 000 words and the publisher who was interested did some editing and suggested I talk to other fathers as well. I talked to one. I then lost the recording of the conversation. And I was busy with work. Editing a magazine. Then my daughter was born.

The second book was a business book. It was, and still is, an idea in my head. Why did I add 'in my head'; it wouldn't be an idea in my toe, would it? The book was 'Business Lessons from My Children'. It was going to be short, quirky, beautifully designed and powerful. I still like the idea. Who knows, perhaps I will actually do it one day.

Book number three. My father – there he is again – lived a phenomenal life and I always felt his stories needed to be shared with the world. I bought him a voice recorder and asked him to record memories and thoughts on it, which I would then transcribe. I had also promised to spend more time with him in Maseru, talking, reflecting and recording those conversations, also for transcription. We could then find a way of turning it into a coherent and comprehensive memoir.

None of that ended up happening. In the meantime, he said he would start writing it and, once completed, we could look for a publisher or publish it ourselves. My father probably wrote hundreds of thousands, if not millions, of words in his time as an academic and as a management consultant. By hand. I suspect that's where the writing gene came from.

He transitioned in December 2016. He spent two weeks with us in Joburg early that November. Every day during his visit, he spent time sitting on the patio, reading and writing. The week after his death, I went through his desk, looking for the book and found that he had only put together a table of contents, with some basic notes here and there but not enough to turn into a memoir.

When he was training me to work on proposals, reports and the like, he always said the most important thing to put together was the table of contents. It would obviously change as one wrote, but it gives structure to thinking. His table of contents wasn't really useful for me. I would have preferred that he had written parts of the meat of the book instead. So, I decided my third, but actually first, book would be about him and his life, 'Through My Eyes'.

The fourth book was strongly suggested to me by my tarot reader – I have been seeing her for close to twenty years, hence the feelings of ownership. She remarked, during a reading, that the feelings of being an outsider that I have always felt, even in my own family, are feelings that so many other people experience. So, what would be perfect would be a book about being an outsider. My working title was 'On the Edges, Looking In'.

And now, here we are. With this book. My first, fifth book. The book I have written to get people off my back and to tell stories. My stories. While the others were clear in their intention, this one isn't. I hope that, by the end of it, it will be. I wrote it to get the monkey off my back. I started writing this without a plan, without a specific intention. I simply focused on putting words on the page. The only hope is that it makes something easier, or clearer, or simply entertains at least one person.

I learned that the hard way. Jumping off a poetry stage, having shared a five-minute performance poem that took weeks to write and weeks to memorise, the reaction would be, 'such and such line was amazing'. And I would think, all those words, all those thoughts, all those feelings and all you connected with was a particular line? I learned that it's all right. As long as you walk away with something that adds value to your life, however big or minuscule.

Anyway, let's get started.

LIKE FATHER, LIKE SON

Breaking the cycle

EPIPHANIES ARE crazy things. Have you ever stared at something so long that it blurred and then vanished into the background? Or perhaps that's just familiarity borne out of being too close to things. Or perhaps we just take things for granted and gradually lose sight of them. And then, when something happens that brings it to the fore again, it is labelled epiphany.

As a father, I spend a lot of time stumbling along, hoping I am doing things kind of right but not willing to let up because my children's futures are at stake. Even when I am putting pressure on my children, especially my son, I am often carried down whatever path I step onto like a leaf on a raging river. I feel in control but also out of control. Occasionally, a voice will try to stop me, but I am already well on my way, committed and all that. It is only later that I promise myself to think first, and do better, and handle things better, until the next time.

I wish this was about how I am getting better. It isn't. I don't know if I am getting better or worse at being a father. Whenever it feels like I have a handle on things, my children will flip it on me, but I can comfortably say I am constantly trying to be better. And then Master Yoda's words to Luke Skywalker in The Empire Strikes Back pop into my mind, 'Do. Or do not. There is no try.' Obviously, Yoda never had children.

I'm sitting with my son the one day after having given him a lecture and reflecting on how much he is like me. The disagreements we have are strikingly similar to the ones I used to have with my father, especially as a teenager. I was remembering how, in my twenties, I had to come to terms with being my father's son. I found myself having discussions with people and pushing a particular point of view that my father had pushed on me and how, at the time, I would push back. Now that's my stance.

My father's biggest gripe with me was what he called my constant desire to reinvent the wheel, which was basically his way of saying I should just listen and not argue because his experiences had given him a certain element of wisdom that I could learn from, as opposed to rebel against.

It was always entertaining watching people meet my father for the first time, after having spent time with me. Somehow, I made sense after they talked to my father. The apple didn't fall far from the tree. A chip off the old block. Like father, like son. All these idioms apply to me.

I am a mini version of my father. The way I think. How I view and interact with the world. Some of my mannerisms. Elements of my personality. When I was a teenager, I rebelled. I was my own man – whatever that meant. My father's views were old-fashioned and outdated. In other words, I was a typical teenager. I started my working career at about twelve years old at my father's consulting company. I began with odd errands like fetching the post, going to the bank, etc. As I transitioned from high school to university and then working full-time, I rose through the ranks, eventually doing research and running one of the family businesses. When my father and I disagreed, it was usually related to methodology – my reinventing the wheel – and it often ended up very heated. I remember it got so bad the one day that my father fired me – told me to go home and not come back. I went back to my office and carried on as normal.

I grew older; I started becoming him. At first, I fought it. Fervently. Later I gave up and embraced it. It was inevitable. Being my father is not that bad a thing to be. He was that kind of father. All my friends thought he was cool, accessible and easy to talk to. The clashing was because I am a reflection of him. It took me embracing him in me to recognise how blessed I am to have had him.

And it took the birth of my own son, Kweku, for me to truly understand my father and to make sense of our relationship during my formative years, and it was in a moment of random reflection on both relationships that I had an epiphany.

While Kweku is still young, it is very evident that the idioms that applied to me as a son apply to him as a son – with one significant difference. My father grew up without his mother and I grew up without my mother.

First, my father. From the story he told me not long before he passed away, he lived with his father and his father's wife. He was under the impression that his mother had died and so never looked for her. Early into his teens, he ran away from home (a small fishing village called Elmina) to go to the capital city of Accra. I still can't get my head around a young teenage boy leaving home in the 1940s' Gold Coast, during colonialism, to find his own way in the world.

Anyway, in Accra, he met someone who said they knew his mother, who was living in Kumasi, about 200 kilometres away. He boarded a bus to Kumasi and arrived on my grandmother's doorstep. She had another family. As he told it, while it was amazing to finally meet his mother, it was too much for him and, after a month, he returned to Accra where he eventually went to school. He lived off the goodwill of others and hard work. My father was never very open about the past, particularly his time growing up, fending for himself, but I do know that he eventually had a relationship with my grandmother because there are pictures of us visiting her when I was a baby.

All of this shaped the man he became. He always emphasised the importance of being self-sufficient and independent to a fault. This has held me in good stead, mostly, but has also held me back at various stages of my life. I had to learn, later in life, how to ask for help when I needed it. Although I have become better at it, it is still uncomfortable at times. And, while my father was my only parent for most of my life, and he raised all five of us – I have an older sister, Grace, and two younger brothers and a younger sister, Kweku, Kobina and Efua – to the best of his ability, not having a mother had an impact on his relationships and his approach to parenting.

And me? My mother passed away in a car accident when I was fourteen months old. I do not remember her at all. My younger siblings' mother was my mother from when I was five until I was about fifteen. My older sister

– from my father's first marriage – was also a mother to me, but, for most of my life, she was at boarding school, then at university, then living her life. This impacted on my relationships with girls and women, in particular.

I will never forget the day a friend in high school, in a fit of anger, told me that I wasn't looking for a girlfriend, I was looking for a mother. It stung because it carried an element of truth. Over the course of my life, I have been fortunate enough to have women who played the mother role in various moments, but I also realise that there are certain areas of my life that have lagged emotionally because my mother died.

I was once commissioned by *True Love*, a women's magazine in South Africa, to write a column for Mother's Day. It was one of the hardest articles I have ever had to write, and it ended up being a mini-lecture to those who don't appreciate their mothers.

One thing I am learning is that to push those feelings of inadequacy onto my son is doing him a disservice and I have to allow him his experiences and his journey. He has his mother. And I have to also allow her to bring her uniqueness to the experience of raising our son. I do not have all the answers and, often, the answers I have aren't sufficient. There has been many a moment when I don't know how to deal with something, whereas she does. Being a father is important to me. I consider it one of the most significant roles that I have to play in this life. It is a responsibility, and it is a blessing. And it is a partnership with my children's mother, and my wife, Estelle.

That is the beauty of having two parents. Hopefully the child gains the best of both parents because this parenting thing is hard and there is no manual, as the cliché goes.

The teller of stories

A PSYCHOLOGIST once said to me, when your child feels like they are in the darkness, don't stand on the edge telling them to climb out, rather climb in with them and help them climb out from there. One of the ways of doing this is by sharing not just your triumphs but also your challenges from your younger years.

Since that day, I have tried to share my stories with my children, especially with my son.

Strangely, it doesn't make me feel as uncomfortable as it should. When I am asked about what advice I would give to young people, my response is to let them know that 'it's not that deep', but this I can't do with my son. He already believes that I blame him for everything and that he can't catch a break with me. At least in the moment that I am writing this. Things change so quickly, who knows what the situation will be in the moment when you are reading these words?

The first time that we properly bumped heads I remembered what he was probably feeling because, for years, as far as I was concerned, my father didn't particularly like me, and I was to blame for everything. At one point, in my mid-teens, I called him Sir – instead of Daddy – for about a year to spite him. I have no idea whether it bothered him, but I came to my senses eventually.

The psychologist, on hearing the story of how the son has become the father to a son like the father, and how history seemed to be repeating itself, albeit with a new character thrown onto the stage, suggested that I share more of my stories with my son. She encouraged me to share stories of my journey from boy to man, grappling with all the insecurities that came with the transitions and constantly trying to make sense of the world, especially as a boy who would cry when angry and when sad, and as a teenager and young adult who would cry when angry and when sad.

So, I have started to tell him stories. Sometimes I suspect it becomes a bit much for him. Who wants a father who has a story for anything and everything, loves telling stories and always gets the last word when you are like the father and you want to get the last word in yourself?

Sadly, that is the one element I cannot relate to. I don't know what it is like to have a father who constantly references the past. My father was not a father like my son's father, who, when he was telling his father about a 'drug workshop' at school run by people who were former drug addicts who had been to rehab, said, 'Well, I was also in rehab, before you and your sister were born.' Yes, this is a passing conversation I had with my son. For a couple of seconds, he was truly speechless, especially because I was so nonchalant about it.

Anyway, my father was not that father. He engaged in the present. The stories I heard about his past were in the incidental statements he would make. The kind of sentences that, ten minutes later, you were not sure if he actually said it. I remember, I think, when he talked about how the dictator Idi Amin would come and sit at the back of the class randomly while he was lecturing at Makerere University in Uganda. And how he learned how to make a Molotov cocktail when he was a student in Germany in the 1960s and a member of the African Students Association. And how he left home – my grandfather's home – when he was eleven or twelve or perhaps thirteen years old, I think, and went to Accra from Elmina and was taken in by a young man from his village, who let him sleep on the floor of his one-room living space.

These are memories I have of things he told me, but so much happened in-between that I am never 100 per cent sure about whether I had heard right. We did talk. We talked a lot, although it was generally about what had recently happened, was happening or was going to happen. We talked business. We talked politics. We talked Africa and its history. We talked about how school was, sometimes. We talked sports, especially football and particularly Ghana's Black Stars, Germany's Die Mannschaft, Bayern München and Liverpool.

He never talked about his childhood. He did talk a bit about how he met my mother. He did mention that my maternal grandfather was not thrilled that my mother was in love with a Black man and that it was only after my grandfather passed away that my grandmother gave them her blessing to get married. He would occasionally tell me stories of moments in his life, particularly from his thirties. But he never talked about his childhood.

Children of alcoholics sometimes become extreme teetotallers. This isn't the same, but sometimes I wonder whether I am so open to sharing my stories because my father rarely shared his.

In his later years, he did open up a bit more, although that did not fill in the big gaps. I was 38 when we visited Ghana together with my younger brother Kweku. It was the first time I saw where he went to school and the streets he grew up on as a young teenager, although so much had changed. He showed us the streetlight he used to do his homework under, and where he was standing when Kwame Nkrumah gave his famous Independence Day speech on 6 March 1957. My father had just turned 22 the month before. But not much else.

And so, I tell my children stories. I tell them of my successes but, more importantly, my challenges and my failures. In a way, these pages are an extension of that. I have built a career on the experiences I have had and the lessons I have learned. Anything that I have written over the years for an array of publications, sites and social media have had the seeds of my life experiences in them, however trivial they may be. In my conversations with people, all I really bring is those experiences and the experiences I am going through daily. All I can hope for is that there is something for each person to take and learn from.

These stories are, therefore, for my children, and for you.

How the son became the father

AT THE launch of my poetry books, Voices in My Head and And They Say: Black Men Don't Write Love Poetry, in Johannesburg's city centre in 2015, my father spoke as the guest of honour. Since he had paid for the printing of the main collection, Voices, I thought it was only fitting. Since it was my launch, I performed, but I also had fellow poets performing.

Moving cities or countries is a weird thing because people get to see and live with a version of you that, while still you, can never be the version the people who knew you from childhood know. In the audience, there were a lot of people I had interacted with for a couple of years in my time in Joburg. And the longer my father spoke, the more my thinking, views and way of interacting with the world made sense to my Joburg people. I could see it in their faces.

As a quick sidenote, when I got married, it was important for Estelle to see me in my 'natural habitat', interacting with people and places I had grown up with. So as soon as she could get a passport, we went off to Maseru.

There is a poem by the poet from Trinidad and Tobago, Roger Bonair-Agard, that he wrote for his father. I played it for my father once. If I remember correctly, at the time, he grunted. We were never the most expressive when it came to talking about feelings and love and the like.

Our discussions were often that – discussions. Intellectual forays into everything from African history and politics to business. It was mostly business as I worked with him for a large portion of my life, our bedroom doors facing each other, our offices next door to each other.

Here are some lines from Bonair-Agard's poem:

more and more they say, I am becoming your image, I wonder
if I can keep up your devotion to progressiveness. Remind
myself I too sacrificed many things for an understanding
many will call frivolous ...

someone who has never met you said of me recently, beware
of him, he's just like his father ...

that I would spit their comments back at them like bullets,
if I were worthy enough to shoot on your behalf, if ... as my
shoulders square into yours and my chest expands to mimic
you, I could build a life of work and struggle mentionable in
the same breath as my father ...

pretender to the throne I am only filling out the mandate of
your life ...

The poem ends with, 'Please forgive me, my father, I have become you, inadequately.' From the first time I heard it, I connected with it. It felt like the words I would use if I could ever articulate how I felt about my father. I had tried to write a poem dedicated to him for years, and I still consider what I have written inadequate.

I didn't always feel that way about my father though. I was a sensitive child. Everything was amplified by a hundred, whether good or bad. If I was reprimanded by my father, it was because he did not like me. And everything was my fault. I hungered for compliments and validation from him. There was a part of me that wanted to be liked by everyone, most especially him.

I missed the first signs. Becoming like him, the rebellious 'I'm my own man' blinded me to the signs. Having lived under his shadow in a country and society where I was Frank or Ntate Baffoe's first-born son before I was

Kojo, probably contributed to this. And, when I started to recognise the signs, I fought against them, repeatedly.

It took leaving home, and leaving the business, and leaving the country, at the age of 27, to realise that there was nothing I could really do about this. My father was the cool father amongst my friends, but I didn't see the coolness. With hindsight, I suspect that, for some, I was useful because I provided access to him. I often joked that I was probably a necessary inconvenience for some of my friends and girlfriends to gain that access.

My father trained me. When I was fifteen, I was already doing his research and editing his writing for projects. When I finished high school, after spending a year in Germany as a Rotary Exchange Student, I worked full-time for the family businesses for about eight months before I went to university in Durban, South Africa. When I was at varsity, I used to come home every holiday, even the short ones, to catch up on work. Sometimes, I would come for a weekend to do stocktaking and, when needed, drive to Joburg to buy stock for a shop we had that sold hair products and salon equipment.

At university, I was the annoying student, especially in Organisation and Management and in Marketing. I would argue with the lecturer about the practicality of what we were being taught because I would experiment with ideas every time I went home to work.

I can be a bit tedious sometimes because I struggle to let go of things; that I also get from my father. If I messed up, he would bring it up at intervals, for years, never fully letting go. When I moved to South Africa, he spent ten years trying to convince me to move back home. He would drop a 'you know if you were still here, business would be so much better' randomly in phone conversations. To be honest, it took me a good fifteen years to stop feeling guilty about it.

The signs kept on popping up. I would say something to someone and hear my father's words coming out of my mouth. Literally.

Sadly, Kweku has borne the brunt of it, although I do work hard at being better. It took becoming a father for the first time for me to truly understand my father. To truly understand that, no matter how much I messed up, he would always love me and be there for me. The funny thing is my father lectured me on how hard I was on my son, meanwhile I was simply channelling him.

There is so much of me that I see in Kweku. He enjoys being on his own, chilling at the house. He is introverted but social with those close to him. He has his sulking moments when he withdraws. It really is like looking in a mirror, especially with our disagreements and conflict echoing the disagreements and conflicts I had with my father.

After a brief counselling session for him, the psychologist said to me that they hope that Kweku will, when he is older, understand that his father is doing the best that he can, always. That his father is trying to give him the tools to tackle this life and teach him the values and principles that his grandfather taught his father. I hope so too.

I was blessed enough to have my father live well into my forties and his early eighties. This gave me the opportunity to mature enough to recognise how my father did the best that he could. He was not without fault, none of us is, but I am where I am today because of him, and it is a good place to be.

As I become my father, inadequately, all that I can hope for is that my son will, one day, look back on his life, and our relationship, and come to the same realisation. Sometimes, becoming your father, in whatever way that is, isn't all that bad.

Broken promises

THERE ARE certain promises that we make that, when not fulfilled, seem to linger for an eternity, taking up mental energy and distracting us from the present. When the person we made the promise to passes away, it can be debilitating.

There are a number of promises I made to my father, the first and longest outstanding one had to do with his music, his records specifically. He started collecting in the late sixties and early seventies through to the early nineties when CDs took over. Whenever he travelled, he would pick something up, usually writing the date when he bought the record somewhere on the sleeve. He also did this with books, a habit I have since picked up: date and place where it was bought, even if it is just city.

That record collection is where my love for music was born and has endured. For example, every Sunday morning, from the age of about eleven, I would have to wake up to wash my father's car, come rain or shine, summer or winter. Winters in Lesotho are particularly cold, especially when the chilling wind from the snow-capped Maluti mountain range sweeps down over the lowlands of Maseru. I would use warm water to wash the car, keeping one hand in my pocket and the other in the bucket as much as possible.

Before I headed out with bucket and soap, I would go through my father's collection to decide what I was going to listen to while I toiled. Reggae, jazz, soul, rock and roll, classical, highlife, disco – every genre was featured and I submerged myself in it all. Was today going to be Louis Armstrong, Duke Ellington, Peter Tosh, Bing Crosby, Kori Moraba, Dark

City Sisters, Fela Kuti, Miriam Makeba, Bob Marley, Brothers Johnson, Harry Belafonte, Lou Rawls, Jimmy Cliff, Nat King Cole, Shalamar, Kool & the Gang, George Benson or a random-mix day? Once decided, I would turn the speakers towards the front door, place the needle on the first record and turn the volume up to ensure that I could hear it from the driveway.

I still do that today – spend a couple of minutes before figuring out what the soundtrack will be. I need music to fall asleep; the last thing I do before laying back and reaching for the Sandman's embrace is deciding what music I am going to fall asleep to.

But back to promises. I had made the promise to digitise all my father's records and cut them onto CDs for him so he could continue to enjoy the albums that were so hard to find. He no longer had a turntable in the house and also wanted to be able to play his music in the car, hence the CD. It is mildly fascinating how much technology has evolved in the last few years. We have gone from CD to digital downloads to streaming in a very short period.

I eventually found a turntable that could connect to a computer and record the whole album digitally. When I was home in Maseru for a visit, I grabbed a couple of albums to try out, but they ended up propped up next to the record player, which was still in its box. And then, one day, he was no longer there to give me grief about not 'dubbing his records'.

Dr Frank Baffoe lived a full and rich life. He lived through significant moments and movements over the span of 81 years. When studying colonialism and the British Empire in high school, one day I was struck by the realisation that he was born into a time that seemed so distant yet wasn't – a colonised Africa. I mean, he was a full 22 years old when Ghana gained independence and went from being the Gold Coast to Ghana in 1957 and the Republic of Ghana in 1960.

He lived in Germany from the early 1960s into the 1970s and was part of the African Students Association. He was in an interracial relationship from the late 1960s, in a Europe that was very unforgiving towards such. He lectured at Makerere University in Kampala, Uganda, when Idi Amin was in power. He lived in Lesotho during a time when a lot of activists in the struggle against apartheid were being accommodated in the country, which resulted in two violent raids by the South African Defence Force. My father had friends who were prominent within the Struggle and he visited Cuba in the early 1980s, both of which resulted in him being banned from entering South Africa. I used to push him to write his life story and promised to help him do it.

My father collected books and read extensively, eventually building a library of over 2 000 books. He even had an assistant catalogue them, creating an index and labelling system. In his will, his instructions for me were simple: either donate the books to the library of the National University of Lesotho, on condition that they create a section for them, for example, the Dr Frank Baffoe Memorial Library, within the broader library, or find a way of creating a small space in Maseru for people to be able to access the books.

It is now over four years since he passed away and the books are still sitting in the old house in Maseru. Another promise unfulfilled.

In the early days, after his passing, I carried a lot of guilt and regret for having failed him. Regret can be disempowering and counter-productive. I had to eventually shift my perspective and consider what I did do while he was still alive. And to be frank, it's not like Frank Baffoe is sitting somewhere in the ether ranting and raving about how I never did these things. He would only want me to do the best that I can and not have these things stand in the way. He would understand the challenges that have stood in the way of fulfilling these promises.

The years since he passed have been difficult at times, especially financially. These difficulties stem from projects that we were working on together that we invested in and did not realise their potential. They say life is for the living and I have had to make the decision to focus on living, even if it means not doing the things that I promised him that I would do. I am at peace with it.

His record collection has a special place in my home. I have a turntable and speakers and often listen to them, going back in time, remembering moments and also just enjoying the music that made me love music. He may not have been able to physically and actively write his book, but, in a way, this book is his as much as mine. I am his legacy, as are my siblings, his grandchildren and every person he touched in life. Within these pages are aspects of the story of an African man who had a strong and positive impact globally, albeit often behind the scenes.

There are gaps in each story, but this is my way of filling some of those gaps.

As for his books? I will find a way. One day.

Ode to my children

WHEN MY son was nine years old, I wrote a blog post titled 'Ode to My Son', which was a reflection on the journey that we had travelled to that point. Every time I reread it, I am struck by how every moment before that point in time and every moment since brings with it a newness, as he grows into himself and I learn more about myself because of him.

Have a conversation with a father – at least one who is present – and you will be bombarded with comments on the sleepless nights, the cost of everything from nappies to school and extramurals, the loss of time for self, etc. The responsibility for another human being's life is immense and mind-blowing and takes its own unique toll on you emotionally and mentally. During Estelle's pregnancy, I found that my focus went up while my tolerance dropped, and it became even more extreme after Kweku was born.

Despite the challenges, I consider fatherhood the ultimate blessing. I have never been able to understand the scourge of absentee fathers, which is a problem in South Africa. In a way, my life before children was to prepare me for life after children. I always wanted to be a father. Being raised primarily by my father showed me that parenting is not solely a mother's task and, when I was younger, being a father was always easier for me to process than being a husband.

For my father, family was important, probably because he grew up without family, having to fend for himself. He would always tell us how lucky we were to have siblings. It was also probably why he used to harp on about being independent and self-sufficient; he had to grow up very quickly in difficult circumstances.

As a man, the pregnancy was a little strange. My body wasn't going through changes. I did struggle a bit with morning sickness with Estelle's first pregnancy, which, sadly, ended in a miscarriage in our first year of marriage. We then went through a series of fertility tests and artificial insemination, unsuccessfully, and we had reached the point where we didn't know whether we would be able to have children.

As a result, when she was pregnant with Kweku, there was excitement and anticipation tempered by a real fear that something could or would go wrong. I did feel fragile and emotional at various stages, but everything was happening in her body, not mine. It did become very real, very quickly, when he was born.

I still vividly remember being in theatre, the coolness of the room, the beeps of machinery, the banter between the doctors and Estelle oscillating between telling me not to look – it was a caesarean and I get queasy – and asking for water repeatedly. Holding Kweku for the first time, I felt lightheaded and was sweating profusely. Somewhere there are photos of me sitting on a stool with my head between my knees because, at some stage, it started to feel very hot. I had made the mistake of looking down at Estelle's insides as I walked round the bed to hold my son for the first time.

If there is one place where I felt absolutely useless as a man who considers himself independent, self-sufficient and capable, it was during childbirth. The nurses had obviously been through this so many times; their instructions were always simple and clear. Where I could sit, what my role was, however small, what I should focus on, etc. I felt like an appendix – not really there for anything but with potential to create problems – an unnecessary inconvenience. Once we were back in the ward, I finally felt a bit more useful. They gave me a clipboard to keep track of nappy changes and feeding patterns. I spent the first 24 hours dazed and elated, fearful and happy.

Ironically, when Ayanna was born, I thought I was a pro because I had gone through the process before; plus, it was the same medical team, the same hospital, but there are also photographs of me sitting on the floor, against the wall, my head between my knees. It was so overwhelming.

It was Kweku who made me a father. For four years, before Ayanna was born, he was the one who taught me that, as a father, my job is to love and support my children unconditionally; to guide them while also allowing them the space to discover themselves.

I have learned that having children will teach you about yourself, if you let them. Children have this wonderful way of looking more at what you do than listening to what you say. When my father constantly told me I was capable of achieving anything as long as I put in the effort, I wasn't really listening but rather absorbing it from watching how he lived his life.

I read the books, went for inner-child workshops, went to antenatal classes, was given an incessant stream of unsolicited advice from parents and consumed as much information as I could about raising a child, and then Kweku came into the world to show me that he was a unique individual. What worked in the books would not work with him if I didn't stay open to learning on the fly, using what I gathered from the books as simply a starting point.

The older both Kweku and Ayanna get, the harder it becomes to learn the lessons. When they were babies, all I had to concern myself with was whether they were getting enough sleep, were hungry, needed a nappy change or needed soothing.

Now, even though they are more articulate, they aren't always able to vocalise how they feel or what they want to do. It has forced me to be clear on what my values are because, in addition to providing food and shelter, I want to give them access to all the tools they need to live the lives they want to lead, which won't always be in line with what I think or want.

It is both daunting and exciting, but I wouldn't have it any other way. I am grateful to Kweku for making me a father for the first time. I am grateful to my children for choosing me as their father, for better and for worse. I hope that, one day, they will look back on their lives, and these words, and recognise that I did the best that I could. I wasn't always their favourite person and there were moments of anger, sadness and disappointment, but, overall, my best was good enough.

Another link in the chain

WE ARE each a link in a chain that stretches back through time to wherever the seed of you was planted. We are living representatives of those we descend from. It is a culmination, an amalgamation, a potpourri, our own little melting pot with multiple flavours and spices introduced to the recipe at different points in time.

I use chain to simplify things. It is probably more of an intricate web but, for purposes of this random theory, chain it is. Our responsibility is to carry that lineage forward. Each generation is responsible for ensuring that the next generation starts from a step up. Where my father started from should not be where I start from. And where my children start from should at least be a step higher than the one I started on.

Our names also carry within them a connection to those who begat us. Consider how the griot or praise singer or ordinary human being will speak of a clan, a history, a lineage, a person and their deeds. Within Africa, we are still connected through our names, despite colonialism's attempt to sever that link with 'Christian' names.

But there is so much more to it. To grow up where your people are from is to hopefully have those tales passed down to you. For those of us who didn't, for whatever reason, it becomes a lot harder. There is a word from the Akan people of Ghana – Sankofa. There is also an Adinkra symbol representing Sankofa and it is of a bird facing forward yet looking back picking an egg off its back. Essentially, it means that in going forward, there is merit in looking back and bringing what is good from the past into the present and future.

In my baby photo album, there is a family tree that traces my lineage down to my great-grandparents on both sides, and yet the chain beyond my father is a little blurry and fades into nothing. My grandfathers passed away before I was born. My grandmothers passed away when I was a baby. My grandparents and great-grandparents are really just names in a photo album.

My father was an only child and my mother had two sisters. Having lived outside of and away from Germany my whole life, my contact with the German side of the family has been very limited, except for my mother's younger sister, Tante Antje, who is my godmother. Not a birthday or Christmas went by without a card from her and, in more recent times, we have connected through Instagram and found that it is the best channel for us. The last time I saw her, my other aunt or my cousins was in 1991 when I was nineteen years old.

The sun was rising gently above the ocean, the humidity in the air dulling its rays in a way that draws your eyes to its centre. While the South African sun is harsh, potentially blinding if you even half look in its direction, the sun in Ghana is soft, particularly at sunrise and sunset.

Off in the distance, a traditional Ghanaian fishing boat cuts through the seemingly gentle waves, the fisherman rowing with a powerful rhythm, unbothered by the slight bobbing of the boat, its nose rising and falling in tandem to each stroke of the oars. I look over at my son and daughter, sitting on a small veranda at the Sankofa Beach Resort in Kokrobite. This is their first trip to their grandfather's land, and it is for a month, for them to get a real feel for the country. While their grandfather is no longer with us to tell them stories of his upbringing in Ghana, I have tried to share what little I know.

They were both born and raised in Johannesburg; it is important for me that they know and understand their heritage and where their people come from.

As I watch the fishing boat, I think back on my own life and the challenges of identity that come with being an immigrant, never having lived in my fatherland and only having visited three times with my father when I was well into my thirties. This is a teaching moment. I point out the boat to them and share the story of how their great-grandfather used to be a fisherman, as far as I could tell from my father's sparse stories. And how, through the sheer force of his personality, their grandfather decided that he was not going to be a fisherman and/or a cocoa farmer. As a result, my life has been different, privileged to a certain extent, and, by extension, they too are living very different lives from the children their age we see in Ghana.

Sadly, the stories I tell are full of gaping holes that leave me – and them – wanting more.

My father was always tight-lipped about his upbringing and family in Ghana. Over the years, he would share snippets in passing and I would hang onto these like the proverbial drowning man and the last straw. When I asked him about the Ghanaian family, he would dismiss me with the belief that, if he opened the doors to family from there, many would try to take advantage. He kept those doors closed.

When Facebook, specifically, and social media, in general, started, I began actively seeking out people from Ghana with the same surname, in the hope that I could piece together that side of the family tree. We argued about this because I told him I was doing it.

After many years going by between his visits, he started spending time in Ghana more regularly and, in 2008, when I was 36 years old, my younger brother Kweku and I travelled there with him. I can now say, without a shadow of a doubt, that there is piece missing in your life when you haven't had the opportunity to see and interact with spaces that your parents grew up in. I had never had my father point out where he went to school, or a neighbourhood he grew up in, or areas he navigated. That is what immigrants miss out on. The familiarity and the context.

On that trip, my brother and I finally got some context. Although Accra had changed a great deal in the half-century since he had left for Germany, it was amazing to see where he grew up.

We also visited Elmina Castle (formerly St George of the Mine Castle) in the village of Elmina, not too far from the more well-known Cape Coast Castle. I later found out that Elmina is where the Baffoes predominantly come from, but I haven't spent enough time there to trace my father's steps backwards.

As a result, my relationships in Ghana are predominantly friendships with people I have got to know over the years and less about family. I do have a couple of cousins with whom I have started building relationships, but the distance is such that I am not able to bring the next links in the chain – my son and daughter – into the fold. As yet.

Live long and prosper

IS IT strange to feel a little disappointed about self-prophecies that do not come true, especially about things like mortality? I always thought I was going to die before the age of 28. I had 'Live fast, die young, have a sexy corpse' and other derivatives scribbled on and in many a high-school notebook, file and folder. Then, one day, in a blink of the proverbial eye, I was standing in a room of about 100 people, gathered to celebrate my 40th birthday, listening to my father talk about how I never thought I would live beyond 28.

And now, well into my forties, with children, my wish is to live long enough to see them grow into adults and maybe even have grandchildren. I have this image that won't go away, of me, lying in a hospital bed, old, surrounded by family – Estelle, children, grandchildren, great-grand-children – peacefully slipping into the ether.

For the first 40 years of my life, there wasn't a lot of death, but, in a sense, the death of my mother, my grandmother and my uncle together in a car accident set the tone for my relationship with death and morbidity. Fascinated by the typical image of the Grim Reaper at an early age, I have always been drawn to skulls, Gothic art, architecture and fashion, the supernatural and generally anything considered 'dark'.

My father probably didn't help, especially in my teens, when he would harp on about how when he died I would be responsible for the family and keeping it together. It kept death top of mind. He also didn't want me to learn how to drive, exclaiming to a friend once that he didn't get why I was in such a rush, considering my mother had died in a car accident. And then

I decided to go and have a series of car accidents, which couldn't have been easy to deal with.

I contemplated suicide often as a teenager and in my early twenties. I once jumped off the roof of the house in the hope that it would kill me, but that was silly because I had done it several times before for fun. I don't think my heart was really in it and it was more a cry for attention. A cry that wasn't heard.

I often felt that I was more trouble than I was worth to my father. When I was nineteen, in 1991, I had my first proper car accident. Driving to the office in the rain, in his car instead of mine, I saw two friends – well, a girl I was trying to get with and her friend – walking out of school and I stopped to pick them up. I did a U-turn, cutting across two lanes to go back in the direction I had just come from, when suddenly a cream BMW 5 Series smashed into the side of the car, sending us into a spin. Father MC's 'I'll Do 4 U' was playing. When I had an accident with the same car, a year later, and wrote it off, the song playing was Boyz II Men's 'End of the Road'. Sadly fitting.

Anyway, I didn't have a driver's licence. When the car came to a stop across the road, the two girls jumped out of the car and disappeared. While I was trying to orient myself and figure out what had happened, a man screamed profanities at me through the driver's window, which was now glassless, and he disappeared as well. I would later discover that he had been in the other car and there was a young girl standing in-between the seats. She had smashed into the windscreen and he had rushed her to the hospital. I was taken to the police station where an array of uncles and aunts spent a couple of hours trying to get me released. My father was away in Zimbabwe on business.

I wrote my father a letter, which I left on his pillow for when he returned. In it, I basically said I thought it would be better for all concerned if I was out of his life because I kept on messing up and disappointing him. When he came back, he did two things. The first was to write a response telling me that I was being silly. The second was insisting that I drive. The more I drove, whatever apprehension I may have had about getting behind the wheel dissipated.

I would go on to have two more car accidents and disappoint my father countless times, but it took me having children to understand how a parent's love does not – and should not – diminish despite the challenges our children put us through. Love is truly unconditional when it comes to our children.

Having children also ended my death wish absolutely. I need to be here for as long as possible, to raise and guide them for as long as it takes for them to grow into themselves and the lives they want to lead.

Photographs

IN SOME quarters, as photography spread across the world, photographs were feared because it was believed that they captured the spirit of the subject. We went from that to documenting our lives incessantly with photographs. If you want to see how far we have come, try explaining what photography looked like in the 1970s, 1980s and 1990s to a child who has grown up with cameras on just about any device.

There was the process of buying a film that could take either 12 or 24 photos, and the delicate act of putting it into the camera without exposing the film and therefore ruining the first couple of photos taken or wasting an entire roll because you didn't put it in right. Pointing, with your eye looking through the small window, framing your image and clicking the button, all the while hoping that what you are seeing is what comes out in the two or so weeks it would take for the photo shop to develop the pictures.

There was a certain anticipation, like in the lead-up to Christmas when the gifts are under the tree but you have to wait for Christmas morning (in my family) to actually open them.

My father would come home with the developed pictures and we would stand around, instantly taken back to the moments when the photos were actually taken. I was often the cameraman, so many a time I wouldn't be in the actual picture, but knowing that I was there without being there was a source of pride for me.

Photographs have always been special for me. The foundation of my relationship with my mother resided in the photo albums that she had put together before her passing, her life frozen in a series of mainly black-and-white pictures from her childhood and colour snapshots of her life with my father and me.

For years, she was the woman in the photographs, without voice, without movement, without scent. I would often look at them and try to imagine what she was like. In the pictures with the two of us, it has often felt as if there is a distance between that child and me, the child who had a loving mother ever-present in his life versus the man who has lived a lifetime without a mother. There is a picture of me when I was about one at what looks like a garden party in Uganda. I have it stuck on the wall above my desk in my home office. I am standing in the middle of a crowd of people, alone.

Others who have seen the picture have remarked that it looked like I was the centre of attraction. All I see is loneliness, perhaps because that loneliness lingered for most of my life, like a bad taste remaining at the back of your mouth.

Perhaps, in all of this are the seeds of why I don't enjoy having my picture taken, which has been aggravated in the time of the selfie. I prefer to take the pictures. And Kweku is the same. After being a willing model as a toddler, the older he becomes, the harder it is to get him to be in front of the camera. I often have to beg, cajole or threaten. With all the pictures I take sitting in the cloud, I wonder what my children's relationship with photographs will be. I do hope that they will house memories and be there for them to look back on our lives with a joy, without the melancholy that I have when looking at pictures of my mother, and now my father. My father didn't take a lot of photos in his later years and now he too is frozen in time. As the distance in time grows since he passed, the memories of his voice, his handshake, his laughter, his scent, are all fading and all I have are the photographs.

The value in the sentimental

ON MY eighteenth birthday, my father poured me a shot of Cinzano and gave me a short talk on becoming a man. I don't remember anything that he actually said. I was focused on sipping the alcohol with a straight face; I couldn't tell him that I had tried it before and found it too sweet. It would mean revealing that I was already a regular sipper of booze. At the time, I was partial to screwdrivers (vodka and orange juice).

My father also gave me a ring. It was an ordinary gold ring. A little lopsided with what looked like cracked, hard, deep red plastic in lieu of a jewel/stone. My father said it had belonged to his father, my grandfather. It was the only connection that he, and I, had to him. I made the commitment to pass it onto my son, if I had one, when he turned eighteen. It would be a symbol of that branch of the family tree. My intention had also been to have it set with a beautiful stone or jewel when I could afford it.

And then it was gone.

We had friends over for dinner on a Saturday night and, after everyone had left, I sat at the dining-room table to get some work done. I climbed into bed just after midnight, leaving my laptop, ring and favourite pen on the table. At about 2 am, I woke up because the room was bright. Thinking it was already morning, I sat up in bed to find a man standing at the foot of my bed with a gun. He told me, calmly, to lie down, close my eyes and not move, which I did, covering my head with the bedding. I moved my arm slightly because I wanted to put it over Estelle – I wasn't sure whether she was awake or not – and he tapped me on the ankle with the gun, repeating his instructions.

All the while talking, he moved around the room, going through stuff. I remember lying there wanting to ask him who he was and why he was in my bedroom. I couldn't get my head around what was going on. He then said that he was going to the other room and would be back. As soon as he left the room, I jumped up, slammed and locked the door. Estelle also jumped up; it seems she had woken up before I had and had been lying in silent panic the whole time.

We climbed out of the small en-suite bathroom window and ran down to the security gate of the complex. By the time they got to our place, he was long gone, back over the boundary wall near our unit. He got away with two laptops, four cellphones, some jewellery, my pen and my ring.

The experience was traumatic. We went for one counselling session. Your relationship with home, your personal space, changes when someone breaches it. That is the hard part to deal with, that and the loss of the irreplaceable. While the laptops, phones and jewellery were extremely costly, I have been able to replace them many times over since then. I have never been able to replace the ring. Even my wedding band was stolen, but that is replaceable and I have had two since 2006 when this happened.

Sadly, what is done is done and I can't really do anything about it. I think about that ring often. It not only connected me to my father but to my grandfather as well. Its value to the person who took it would never come close to the value it had for me.

In these days of minimalism, decluttering and Marie Kondo, I wonder whether I am overly sentimental about random items. I have T-shirts that I have owned for 30 years that I can't bring myself to get rid of. I have papers sitting in boxes that I will never use or refer to again, yet they are still in boxes, in my possession. I have magazines and clippings from magazines and newspapers I have written for. I have old cassettes and VHS video tapes that I can't use because I don't have a cassette player or a video machine.

Once again, I blame my father. After he passed away, I spent hours going through bus tickets, airplane ticket stubs and brochures dating back to the 1960s. He had piles of newspaper clippings from the preceding decade, as reference materials for when he wrote. I threw most of it away, although there were some things that I couldn't bring myself to discard and they have been added to my pile of stuff.

One would think that losing something as precious as my grandfather's ring would teach me that one does survive, but I still continue to hang onto so much, for sentimental reasons. Hopefully Kweku and Ayanna will be better with this, and get rid of stuff, when I am no longer there.

The phone call

IN AN interview for a television show, I was asked what technological advancement I considered the most important. The obvious things initially popped into my head – the internet, the smartphone, laptops, etc. And then it hit me – the aeroplane. Without the aeroplane, Frank, a young Ghanaian man, working for the Government Printing Press in Accra, would not have been able to travel to Germany so easily to do an apprenticeship. And everything that followed would not have happened.

Without the aeroplane, he wouldn't have gone to work as a supervisor at a summer camp on an island in the North Sea off the coast of Germany, where he was to meet a young German woman, Elfi, fall in love, and eventually marry, after he got divorced from his Ghanaian wife and mother to his first-born daughter, Grace.

They wouldn't have settled together in the city of Munich and had a baby boy, yours truly. Serendipity or fate, I have always believed that, clichéd as it sounds, everything happens for a reason.

Being a father in this era of exponential technological advancement is not easy. I have always been interested in technology, particularly in the personal realm, and, for a long time, I was the more technological advanced in my home. For my children, this is the norm and they are finding ways to navigate that is both fascinating and a little scary. My job is to protect them, but, at times, I feel like I am being left behind.

While the plane played a significant role in my existence, it is the telephone – from the days of the rotary phone through to smartphones – that has been critical in my relationships throughout my life. Being introverted, it has always taken me time to warm to people, but if there is one thing I can do it is to talk, although I am miserable at small talk.

In my single days, I eventually realised that, when I met someone potentially interesting in the club, the most important thing for me to procure was her phone number, especially if there was a chemistry. I knew that a week or two of chatting on the phone was all I needed to get in her good graces.

When on the phone, all you have is your voice and your thoughts. It is said that the highest form of intimacy is being able to sit in another's presence and not say anything. On the phone, it is even more intimate. The person's voice is in your head, even when they aren't speaking. Sometimes it is enough to know that the person is on the other side.

After I left Lesotho to move to Joburg, my relationship with my father was reduced to extended phone conversations. Prior to that, it was just the two of us at home for a couple of years and we would sit and have long conversations that centred primarily on work, politics and social issues, but mainly work. It took a few years for him to accept that I wasn't going to move back to Lesotho, particularly after I got married, and our conversations evolved. We would still vent about business problems and money, but we would also talk about the kids, football, politics, and the like. While I only had fourteen months with my mother, I had 44 years with my father. I served as his sounding board and also depended on him greatly for advice and guidance.

There was not a single professional decision that I did not talk over with him, even if it was to simply break down my reasoning behind a decision. To be honest, I usually had my mind made up when I talked to him, but it was always good to have someone to listen.

The last time I heard my father speak was on the phone. He had been sick off and on for a couple of months. He was hospitalised for a few days in October 2016. In November, he spent three or so weeks with us and it was wonderful to just have him in our space. I still have the blurry pictures he took of my daughter climbing the window burglar bars, as she was hanging out with him in the mornings. He would sit outside on the patio at a plastic table, with his little portable radio playing BBC Africa, and write. He would take tentative walks around our complex with Estelle and the kids. I would have to help him into and out of the shower and wake up every four hours to take his blood pressure. Little did we know that this would be our last time in his presence.

He went back home to Maseru and took a turn for the worse about ten days before he was due to leave for Ghana for Christmas. I don't think he actually wanted to go. I maxed out my credit card to pay for his ticket; it was the least I could do.

Fast-forward to the morning of Tuesday, 13 December, and the phone call with him. He was back in hospital – well, actually a clinic in the town of Maputsoe, about a 45-minute drive from Maseru, which was run by a Ghanaian doctor. It only had one private room, which is where he had been in October when I had driven to Lesotho as soon as I heard he was in hospital. I called him that morning in December at about 11 am. He sounded tired. My last words to him were, 'Get some rest. I will talk to you later.'

In her book *Before Forever After*, Helena Dolny talks about giving people permission to leave the physical realm. I often think that those last words were my giving him permission. He had held on for a long time.

About two hours later, I received a phone call from his wife, whom he had married seven years prior, frantic, crying, incomprehensible. Someone from the hospital came on the line to say the doctor was with him but it wasn't good. I kept asking, 'Is he gone? Is he gone?' He was. At least physically.

There were two people I talked to on the phone all the time. My father and my closest friend Gerrard. When my father transitioned, it all fell on Gerrard's shoulders. We would often talk two to three times a day, sometimes for at least an hour each time. He was my sounding board. I would get into the car and call him, drive to my destination, arrive and sit in the car for another fifteen minutes talking. I would call him when I walked out of wherever it was, regardless of time, and talk on the drive home, once again sitting in the driveway to finish our conversation.

From the balcony of his apartment, you could see glimpses, through trees, of William Nicol Drive, a main road in Johannesburg. Nearly every time I drove on that road, I would phone him and tell him to wave. We would end up on the phone for the next hour. We never ran out of things to talk about.

On the afternoon of 18 January 2019, we had a meeting in Sandton. After the meeting, we walked around the mall a bit and then split up with the intention of meeting the following day with another friend. Gerrard was going to a braai (barbecue) with his fiancée that evening so was going home to refresh before fetching her.

I was riding my motorcycle and don't use my phone when riding. When I got home, there was a long voice note briefing our friend on what happened in the meeting, which he was to have attended, and reconfirming our meeting for the following day. I listened to it with irritation because I am not a fan of voice notes. Later that evening, sitting on my patio, having a drink and a cigar, watching a film or something, a call came in. I didn't know the number, so I let it ring. A few minutes later I checked my messages and there was a WhatsApp message from Gerrard's fiancée asking me to call her. I called immediately and she asked me to go to his place urgently but wouldn't tell me why.

I jumped into the car, phoned the missus, who was out at dinner with friends, to let her know what was happening. We arrived a few minutes apart because she had been phoned and was told that Gerrard had passed away. From that moment until the following Saturday, I was on my phone constantly as we prepared for his memorial and funeral, as people around the world found out and wanted to reach out to the family.

I am still not a fan of voice notes and prefer text communication. I have two mobile phones, which rarely ring. When they do, I often let them ring and go to voicemail, even when it is friends; I don't like being forced to speak on someone else's schedule. I have lost the two people I used to speak to constantly on the phone and also seem to have lost my desire to have long conversations on the phone. Perhaps there is a correlation.

I speak

I speak for the boys who have lost their fathers
And know that, while they will never be seen again
They are always there

I speak for the men who love their sons
And do what they can
To give their sons the tools to navigate this world
For when they are lost one day

I speak for the boys who will become men one day
Excited yet anxious, dreaming of that day
When they too shall take up the mantle
And build lives worth something

I speak for the men who were boys once
And look back with nostalgia, hindsight
And wish they could do things differently
While recognising that boyhood is what made them
The men they are today

I speak for the boys who were afraid of the dark
I speak for the men who fear the darkness
Outside and inside

I speak for the boys who sleep without a care
In time they will know how sweet that sleep was

I speak for the men who don't want to sleep
Knowing that tomorrow brings with it burden and responsibility

I speak for the boys
Who wish for an example of what it means to be a man
In a world where everything seems broken

I speak for the men
Trying to be an example of what it means to be a man

I speak for the boys
Who cry themselves to sleep at night

I speak for the men
Who hunger for the release of tears
That never seem to come

I speak for the boys who never feel good enough

I speak for the men who feel they never do enough

Unforgettable

NAT KING Cole's voice and music will forever be engraved in my heart. My father had happy and joyous moments during his life, of this I am sure. Painfully, when I think of the years before his passing, I see more the burden of life, and family, and business. Perhaps it was because, for most of my adult life, I served as his sounding board and so our telephone conversations were an opportunity for him to offload. There was many a time when I came off a call with him feeling a little down, the weight of our collective worlds on my shoulders. In the later years, I made a conscious effort not to share my travails with him every time we talked and tried to focus on the positive.

He loved to laugh and, when he did, it was from the stomach and his eyes would twinkle. He had a distinct laugh that is hard to describe but I knew from a distance. In high school, aged about twelve, I performed – well, I mimed – Michael Jackson's 'Billie Jean' in the school revue. I had the hair, the jacket, the gloves, the pants that ended just above the ankle and the white socks. I had the steps from the performance Michael did at Motown's 25th anniversary down pat and then, from the audience, my father started laughing. It may have been out of joy and pride, but when you are a teenager all that you feel is embarrassment. And the steps went out the window. I stumbled through the performance and couldn't get off the stage fast enough. Fortunately, on the second night, when he wasn't there, I was able to demonstrate my mastery as a Michael Jackson impersonator.

It was probably also one of the last times he had the time to come and watch me in a school activity, although we didn't have many.

When Nat King Cole came on, he couldn't help himself. He would smile and, to my chagrin, sing out loud, loud. I always wondered what memories the music held for him. When you are young, you don't think to ask your parents their stories, or at least I didn't, waiting for him to tell them if he felt like it.

A few years after his transition, one of my favourite musicians, Gregory Porter, did a cover album, *Nat King Cole & Me*. Porter said how, for him, Nat King Cole was like the father he never had. For me, Nat King Cole's music, the richness and warmth of his voice, is a receptacle for the memories of the father I had. And my children had to go through my misguided attempts at singing along with Gregory Porter to the music that Grandpa absolutely loved.

I love you

THERE IS a power in words and the most powerful words that can be spoken are 'I love you', and yet, for many of us, they are the hardest to utter, with meaning. In high school, they were the words we used to ask a girl to be your girlfriend. It was a way of discovering what the words meant to you; when you discover 'real love', you also realise that, in the times that you have used them before, it didn't feel like this.

As a boy becoming a man, the funny thing is that the only time you express love for a male friend is when alcohol is involved.

It hasn't been, and still isn't, easy for me to express love verbally. I often wonder why that is. Perhaps it is because I come from a family that isn't particularly affectionate, especially verbally. Also, I grew up in an environment where love is shown by one's actions rather than one's words. The first time I told my father I loved him was on New Year's Eve in 2000. I had spent Christmas with my family in Maseru and came back to Joburg the day before New Year's Eve to party.

I had a couple of drinks in me and phoned my father earlier in the evening to wish him a happy new year before the cellular networks became overloaded. As I was saying bye, I slipped in a quick 'I love you'. He mumbled 'I love you' back, more than likely thrown off by the anomaly in our conversation, and we both hung up.

I don't remember any other occasion when either of us verbalised our love for each other. It is a regret that lingers, and I often wonder why neither of us felt comfortable speaking the words, considering we both had a love for and worked with words, understanding their importance and power. I know that he knows I loved and appreciated him. After he passed away, the doctor who treated him and was with him in his last moments told me that my father had said he appreciated the love and support I gave him, especially in his later years.

Although I still struggle with it, I have become better, influenced by Pam, my aunt – and mother – in Joburg, but it is confined to her and a handful of people. I never told Gerrard that I loved him, even in passing, and that is another regret. I don't say it enough to Estelle, to my children. I try to show it daily but have to keep reminding myself that there is a power in words, especially those words.

The death of boredom

THE CYCLICAL nature of life is such that our children will sometimes find themselves in similar situations to the ones we experienced growing up. Even understanding this makes it hard to create a different experience for them.

In my early teens, I would get dragged to extended family gatherings where there would be no children my age. Often, they would either be younger than I was or older, at a time when a difference of three to four years either way made it hard to connect. I would spend a lot of time on my own daydreaming or would be recruited into handling the braai while my father held court, in-between giving instructions on the cooking of the meat. It was probably easier for me to handle the solitude amidst the madding crowd because my brother Kweku is five years younger than I am and my sister Grace is eleven years older. So even at home, I would entertain myself, spending a lot of time in my head and in my room.

My son Kweku, in some ways, mirrors that, although, fortunately, he does have age-mates in our circle of friends. We have ended up at gatherings where, if there aren't age-mates, he is the only boy. He also has the same awkwardness or discomfort I had with new spaces and new people, so, even when there are other children his age, it takes him time to connect. While Ayanna can also be shy in new spaces, she finds it easier to connect with other kids, even when she's the only girl.

I am still not very good at breaking the ice. Making random small talk is uncomfortable. When they were younger, doing the kids' birthday-party circuit needed me to psyche myself up and I spent many a birthday party chilling on my own, at my child's beck and call because I struggle to work the room and connect with other parents.

As Kweku grows older, it does feel like technology makes it easier for him to be in new, unknown spaces because he just finds a spot and buries himself in his phone, playing games, watching videos and chatting to his friends. While a part of me is glad that he has something to occupy himself with, I do worry that it also serves as a crutch because he isn't forced to navigate socialisation. I also try not to force friendships in the way that it was done to me. I will insist that they meet with other children in the space but also let them sit with us until they feel comfortable enough to interact some more.

Yet, they never seem bored in the way that I was. And with boredom comes the exploration of self and the edges of your creativity. While I recognise that being stuck in your head constantly is not always conducive to navigating the world, it is important to be with yourself, bored, trying to figure out how to entertain yourself. This applies to whether you are out or at home.

Technology, while necessary and very much a part of our lives, fills in all the gaps and serves as a distraction. I see my children struggling to entertain themselves when there is no WiFi, or electricity, because they can't sit on their devices. Reading, painting, writing, playing with non-electronic toys doesn't even cross their minds. They would rather sit and moan about not being able to go online. I try to be an example for them, spending my time reading or colouring in or doing something else that doesn't involve technology, but it doesn't seem to click with them.

Worst of all, I am partly to blame because I am the one who has brought all this technology into the house; I enjoy interacting with it as much as they do, whether it is playing games on a console or my phone, spending time on social media or watching movies and series. Plus, I don't want them to be left behind as technology fully permeates all aspects of our daily lives.

I spend my days oscillating between being the device policeman and being the overly accommodating father. It can be so tiring.

So many tears

WE, ESPECIALLY as men, are taught to hold our emotions, to approach the world with a stoicism that borders on cold, calm and calculated, even when, on the inside, there is turmoil. You learn to suck it up and get on with it, regardless of how much it actually hurts. Sometimes, most times, you are able to do it. Sometimes, other times, it breaks through the walls you have created and manifests in ways that are not particularly constructive. Some of the addictions I have battled with over the years, including alcohol and drugs, bear testament to this, at least for me.

I have come to the conclusion that I am a crier and yet I can count the number of times, probably about five, I have properly cried in the last decade. Three of those times were when my mother-in-law, my father and my best friend died. I bawled my eyes out and, in a way, felt better for it. Getting it out of my system.

Occasionally, I will have a couple of tears watching a movie, or reading something, but those moments are few and far between, helped by my defaulting to mainly action films as a form of escape from all the things I have to deal with. I have been wired so tightly for so long that it takes moments of so-called weakness for the tears to creep out.

I used to cry when I was angry, in my teens and my twenties. The anger would build, and the tears would flow. I haven't lost my temper or become really angry in years, which is probably a good thing because I do have a temper; one of those seeing-red-regret-everything-I-said-after tempers.

I never finished watching the film *The Pursuit of Happyness* featuring

Will Smith. Based on the real-life story of Chris Gardner, there is a scene where Gardner and his son are homeless, sitting in a public toilet stall, with someone banging on the door. The sheer anguish in Will Smith's face. I stopped watching.

At the time, Kweku was about six months old and I understood the pain of not being able to look after your family; I had flashbacks to growing up. It is also one of my biggest fears since I had children. It was a definite crying moment, but, as a father, those are the moments when you have to suck it up, no time for crying. I think.

I never saw my father cry. I watched him go through life experiences that would have broken most and don't remember ever seeing him cry, not even shed a solitary tear. In disagreements, he would tell me to take emotion out of the discussion and state my case calmly and, I felt, coldly.

The rationality and logic of my thought processes were more important than how I felt. I could never get it right, keeping my emotions in check. I am much better at it now. I don't know if that is a good or a bad thing.

This is not an indictment of my father. He was who he was because of the life he lived. I lived with him long enough to understand that he was not perfect and that, sometimes, he needed to power through a great deal just to ensure that we could have the life that we had. Being a parent to five children and running his own business, with staff who also depended on him, meant that there was rarely time for cracks.

Strangely, I hope that he had those moments to break down, even if it was when he was alone in his room. My children have seen me cry but perhaps not enough. And I have not always been the most accommodating when they have cried, which, I realise now, is not fair.

It is funny how the only time we, as men, seem to let down our guards is when we are drunk. The alcohol makes the walls a little soggy and emotion will seep through. All that repressed emotion scrambling to find even the tiniest of releases. All of a sudden, it is arms around each other, 'I love you' tumbling out of slurring mouths at will. It is all so comical and tragic, at the same time. Somehow, personal space and the illusion of masculine decorum go out the proverbial window and we are honest with each other, for a brief moment.

Sometimes, a good cry is all you need. And afterwards, you wipe the tears and get on with it.

Easing the pain

He is silent
Because
When he speaks
The tears come
Raging
From the darkness
That he keeps at bay
Most times

Living a dream deferred

CHILDREN COME with sacrifice. At the same time, children need to see us living our lives to the fullest. While what-ifs are an exercise in regret, especially when applied to our own lives, I have often wondered what my father's life trajectory would have been like if he hadn't ended up an entrepreneur in Maseru, single-handedly trying to build businesses while raising five children. It was in my teens that I realised that a lot of his decisions put us at the forefront and his desires on the back burner.

I wonder what he would have done differently if my mother hadn't died, or if his marriage to my younger siblings' mother hadn't ended in divorce, or if the businesses had flourished from the get-go and he hadn't had to navigate the turbulence of entrepreneurship for most of his life.

He always talked about writing books, primarily non-fiction. He had piles upon piles of newspaper clippings on a range of topics he wanted to write about, from politics to economics and everything in-between, from an African perspective. In the years before he died, he was fascinated by the evolution of institutions and bureaucracy and how, to change society, it needed a change in the systems that drove institutions. It was on his books-to-write list.

He wanted to set up an entrepreneurship institute in Maseru and, at some stage, was exploring creating a pan-African institute in Zimbabwe with some friends and colleagues. He established a magazine called *Business Focus* when I was in high school. It was reborn years later as the weekly newspaper *Southern Star*, which he ran from about 1997 to 2001. It was something that he wanted to revive.

I must have been about eighteen when I discovered that he wrote poetry; he never made mention of it, even when I started exploring poetry as a teenager. I came across a poem in his daily planner. In a way, helping me publish my poetry collection *Voices in My Head* was a way of living a dream through me.

The role of a parent is to create the foundation for their child or children to thrive. It isn't to live vicariously through them, pushing them to do the things that we wish we could have done. When I look at the list of things my father wanted to do that he didn't, because he had to reconcile those with our needs, all I am clear on is that, regardless of what I need to do for my children, they will be better for my pursuing my dreams, however big or small, because they benefit from it materially, mentally and spiritually.

Sacrifice, yes; defer all dreams, no.

Becoming

There was a time
I dreaded becoming
My father

Mentally, intellectually
That boat sailed
In my twenties
Disappeared over the horizon
In my thirties

In my forties,
It is my body that follows
His trajectory

It wasn't always so
But I accept and embrace
My stomach taking on his softness
My hands slowly wrinkling into his
My cheekbones fading
The vein on his temple
That used to rise up
Whenever he had a headache
Has been transported to mine
My V-shaped torso has become the I
That was his

MOTHER

A car crash

THE OPENING sequence for a film. Screen. Black. Sounds of traffic. The screeching of a car's tyres as the driver slams on the brakes. A loud crash. The violent sound of metal on metal, twisting. Silence. The image starts to fade in. The scene is blurry, gradually becoming clearer. You see a car that has crashed into the side of a truck. The front of the car has crumpled. The windscreen is broken. A baby, still strapped into his baby seat, lies face down on the road, blood from his forehead slowly creating a puddle on the tar. Still silence. And then you hear people.

This was the idea I had for the opening sequence of a film script I was going to write. The baby. Me. In the car, my mother, her mother and my uncle. They don't make it. The only one who makes it, outside of the baby, is the baby's nanny, Mary, who is still in the back seat.

I have no idea how the movie would play out from this point forward, but this was always the image I had of the accident in which my mother died. I carried prominent scars on my forehead for most of my life. When asked about them, my standard response was, 'My mother died in a car accident. I survived but I hit the windscreen.'

As a teenager, I found a file at the back of my father's wardrobe. It told the story of the accident and the aftermath. The truck belonged to the Ugandan government and my father sued them, on my behalf, for negligence. The driver's details were in the file. For a while, I planned to go to Kampala and track him down. Make him pay, somehow, for being the cause of my growing up without my mother.

My father wasn't thrilled when he discovered I had seen the file. The memories were painfully uncomfortable for him. I didn't remember how it felt, waking up in a hospital, without a mother, a grandmother, when, just days before, I was surrounded by maternal love.

Fortunately, I got on with life and forgot my desire to re-enact the movie *Death Wish* – the original with Charles Bronson, not the remake with Bruce Willis, which I have yet to see.

I suspect that pool of blood image came from a document from a university neurologic clinic in Tübingen, Germany, where my father took me two weeks after the accident. In the report, the director, Professor Dr W. Schulte, writes:

> Information about the duration of the child's unconscious state after the accident is very scanty. When the child was brought, he still had plaster on the facial wounds. The child was declared dead by the first eyewitnesses immediately after the accident because he laid in a blood bath. Apparently the unconsciousness did not last very long.
>
> The radiograph is without findings; the child is quite restless and cries in sleep. The father, a lecturer in Economics at the Makerere University, Kampala, flew in with the child for the medical examination.
>
> Up to present the early childhood development has been complete inconspicuous. ECG: (conducted during sleep). No cramp currents, no certain findings about the centre of damage, questionable retardation of the frontal, which should not be seen as sure pathological.
>
> The vater has been told that a permanent change need not be expected, and that the dispositional and the characteristic changes can be explained by the readjustment and the situational changes.

I don't know why, but I find there is a certain charm in the language; a warmth that comes from a relatively clinical reporting of a diagnosis.

After my father died, I collected all his papers and brought them to my home for safe keeping. These papers include the nondescript pink folder filled with accident reports, death certificates, lawyers' letters, court papers, and my father's letters to the court and the lawyers.

Essentially, they screwed us, intentionally or unintentionally. While he was dealing with the death of his wife, mother-in-law and cousin as well as an injured son yearning for his mother, they didn't file paperwork when they were supposed to and the case came to naught.

At some stage, when I was in my twenties, he told me how he wallowed in drink for some time afterwards, coming home from work inebriated and passing out on the bed, with me playing in the darkened room. It was Mary who snapped him out of the abyss of self-pity and pain by pointing out how I now depended on him solely to raise me, to be both father and mother.

I have no memories of this period. Sometimes I wonder whether I blocked it out because my memories of childhood start from around age five. There is nothing before that but snippets of stories and pictures from moments I think I remember. Sometimes I wonder whether that is for the best. A black hole I don't have to deal with.

A picture

Her picture hangs
on the wall above my bed
Her eyes are shuttered
A gentle smile
Tastes her lips
Soul peers through
The crack in her vision
From beyond the surface
Of her likeness
She watches me
Passing perpetual judgement
Speaking endless love
Giving forever encouragement
When I leave the room
Her image stays engraved
On the inside of my pupils
Her voice unknown
Whispers to me
Her heart pounds in my chest
I am her manifestation
Carrier of her dreams
I draw her breath
Cry her tears
Live a continuation

Of her lifetime
When I close my eyes
We blur
Our souls fuse
We become what we will always be
Two wholes of we
Though I live our life
Inadequately

Ten years a mother

I HAD a mother between the years of five and fifteen. My father remarried in Lesotho a few years after my mother died. From what I could gather, I was a shy child, even more so after my mother passed away. I did not warm to people easily, but, from first meeting, I immediately took to the woman 'Me Mokone, who would become my father's wife and the mother of my younger siblings.

She was the woman I called Mummy until, when I was fifteen, her relationship with my father ended and they divorced. Our relationship, at that stage, was tentative, at best. At times, I felt that she placed my siblings, her children, above me and, as a teenager, I was able to distance myself a bit more than I had when I was totally dependent.

The weird thing about the divorce was that it felt as if I was being divorced as well. She moved to a house not too far from our home, where my father lived and had custody of my siblings. I remember on weekends going with my father to drop my siblings off at her place.

We would get there and they would jump out of the car and run to their mother. Even though I wouldn't have, I was never asked if I wanted to stay and so I would sit in the car, watching all of this. Then my father and I would head back home and chill for the day, him usually reading the papers, writing or catching up on work, and I lounging in front of the television.

That, in essence, was the end of our relationship as mother and child, although, in later years, she would refer to me as her child, and we have interacted occasionally, the last time being when my father died. She was there for support as we laid him to rest, giving advice and guidance.

This is what 'mother' has meant to me through my life: women who come into my space, play that role for a period, and then move on, or perhaps I move on.

There was my second host mother, in Germany, who always seemed to know when I needed reassurance, which she would give with a look and a smile. There is my Aunt Pam, who embraced me as her child wholeheartedly when I moved to Joburg, and she continues to be Mom to this day. There was my mother-in-law Elaine, who, until she transitioned in 2013, would take my side over Estelle's most times, and we were lucky to have her living with us when Ayanna was born. There is Gerrard's mother, Charlene, who continues to be a shoulder to lean on.

No one will be able to replace my mother, but I have been fortunate enough to have a mother's love, repeatedly.

The boy remembers

HE REMEMBERS, not quite like yesterday, but enough to feel the pain as a distant twinge in his heart. He was maybe eight, perhaps nine. He stood in the kitchen or perhaps the living room, looking up at her. She was pregnant, in a blue dress, perhaps dark blue, but blue nonetheless. He doesn't remember what she said or what he had done wrong this time, but it didn't deserve what followed.

He did know that this time he wouldn't have to get a stick from the many peach trees outside in the garden. He wouldn't have to go to school with welts on the back of his legs, the result of her taking the stick from the tree, thickish, yet supple. He would not have to listen to it whistle through the dense, tense air. He wouldn't have to listen to his screams, knowing they were coming from him, even though he heard them distantly. He would not have to feel the bite of the soap in the morning, when bathed, before school.

She slapped him.

He fell.

He stood up.

She slapped him again. Something told him that it would probably be better if he stayed down, but he stood up again. She slapped him again. He fell again. He remembers this although he does not remember how many times he got up again. He remembers eventually staying down, curled into himself as she kicked him, and then didn't. He also remembers the little girl standing, watching and laughing.

At some stage, she stopped and left him there on the floor, curled up in a tight ball. He doesn't remember how long he stayed there. He may have slept there. He may have gone to his bedroom, climbed into bed, and slept, deeply.

He remembers the black eye when he woke up and had to go to school sporting a badge of dishonour. He doesn't remember the explanation for that black eye. And the welts on his legs, negligibly hidden by his shorts, on other days. Maybe no one said anything even though they must have seen them.

His father would be home soon. But not soon enough to see the black eye because it had finally faded, as the welts often did, before his father came home. By the time his father had come home, all he would have is memories of the good days that had passed, and he would just be happy to see his father.

Memories have a strange way of being static sometimes. Frozen in time, the way a photograph is. And the child's memory was short. The pain of moments was always temporary, and so he never told his father about those moments when he came back after two, three, four weeks away.

And when he eventually told his father, he was angry and incoherent and raging, and it was not the right time, and time had passed. He was a teenager then. He carried the residues of this pain deep and when he finally talked about it, she was no longer there and it didn't seem important any more.

In later years, he laughed about it. It was what happened to everyone, not just him. The moments became the mark of childhood lived, in all its glory ... and tragedy.

Word speaks

When the earth implodes
When it sucks humans to death at its core
I will be the last thought
The final state of existence
The last word to be spoken

When their lives flash before their collective eyes
When the sins of their fathers, and their fathers,
Come home to roost on the volcano's edge
When regret clogs their arteries
And they dream of taking it all back
I shall be the last word to pass their lips

I take no pride in this knowledge
I do not preen or gloat or swagger
It gives me no pleasure and no satisfaction
I do not linger in anticipation of that moment
When I am spoken in truth
When all that I am and all I represent
Is whispered to the heavens
In the hope that I shall bring hope
In the wish that I may somehow fulfil a last wish
In the belief that the mere mentioning of me
Shall reverse centuries of action

I do not take any pride in all of this
It truly gives me no pleasure
To know that I shall be on the tip of billions of tongues
As mankind slips brutally into nothing

I am the last word to be spoken
I am

mother

Mothering from a distance

WHEN MY mother and my grandmother died, my aunt Antje, who is also my godmother, was still a teenager. She went to live with my other Aunt Regine back in Germany. Living on the other side of the world, I didn't see much of my aunts, but, without fail, every birthday and every Christmas, I received a card from Tante Antje.

Though a small gesture, the impact was immense. It always made me feel part of that side of my family, even though it was only from her. My mother was the eldest of three daughters and I have three cousins who I have only seen once, in 1991, when I was in Germany.

To say that we are distant is an understatement, but now, in times of social media, Tante Antje and I have found each other through Instagram. We tried the email thing for a while, but, with my German being really bad and Tante Antje's English only slightly better, it just didn't work sending one-liners. I admit to using Google Translate a couple of times.

Now, we share thoughts, pictures and the goings on in our respective lives on Instagram. She even has the semblance of a relationship with Estelle. Every time she sends a picture, I realise that she's getting older and the urgency to visit with the family becomes even more pronounced.

Sadly, the one time I visited Germany, I was there on a press trip, spent one night in Stuttgart and due to work wasn't able to take even a few days to go check up on them. Something I still regret.

She remains the only lifeline I have to Germany. One of my greatest fears is something happening to her and not knowing about it, losing that one connection I have to my roots in Germany, where my mother is buried.

Scratch

Sometimes my stories are
Unnecessarily long
But it is the incessant scratching
That make the memories real once more
Times forgotten are like the falling tree in the forest with no witnesses

Sometimes though painful
It is necessary to remember
Because it is in the incessant scratching of the scabs of time
That reveals the truth
As you remember it

I kneel before darkness

Definition of self is fluid
A meandering thought
A wisp of smoke
A drop of water snaking down the window

Moments of clarity are static
A wall to be climbed over
A fire to be extinguished
A madness that needs a cure

I am no longer exact
I no longer seek a response to my cries
I lose my voice
And regain it in moments of silence
My tongue rests while my mind works

Please hold my hand
Console me with triviality
Distract me with pettiness
Speak of nothing meaningful
Help me rest easy
Show me that the purpose of living
Is merely to live and experience

I am tired of purpose and hope and dreams and future and utopia
I crave them not
I seek the chaos of insanity
I wish to return to childhood
To rediscover the beauty of colour
The laughter in sound
I wish to touch the sky with every smile

Make it new again
Please Mother
Make it new again

GROWING UP

My heroes were on the walls

WATCHING A documentary about Muhammad Ali, I was struck by how big an impact he had on me when I was a child. I was eight years old when he lost to Larry Holmes, and I have memories of watching the fight with my father. I was heartbroken because, even at that young age, I could see that Ali was at the end of his career. I read a copy of an early biography of his as a young teenager and, by then, had watched a lot of his earlier fights.

His poster was prominent on my bedroom wall, alongside Bob Marley, Malcolm X, Kwame Nkrumah and Bruce Lee. With hindsight, what I connected with was their ability to live for a cause and be their true selves, regardless of the circumstances or consequences. These were men who had principles that superseded anything and everything else. Malcolm X went from a life of crime to a life of legacy. Bruce Lee carved a path for himself based on a strong belief in his self-worth and the value he brought to the table. Muhammad Ali was willing to give up what he had worked his whole life for and go to jail rather than be drafted into the US army to fight in Vietnam in what he considered an unjust war against people he had no quarrel with. Kwame Nkrumah was a key figure in the independence of my fatherland, Ghana, and the evolution of pan-African ideals.

As I grew older, I found other heroes who all made it onto my wall. Many musicians found a place on that wall, although many of them had a fleeting presence. It was a time when glimpses into their true nature and character were sparse and controlled. Not like today where they lay their lives bare on social media. One thing I did learn was to never watch interviews with my favourite artists. The majority tend to disappoint. It is one thing to hear your life laid bare in lyrics; it is another to watch them struggle to string coherent sentences together or to discover what they truly think about something that you hold dear.

I was fortunate. The home I grew up in was filled with books from the trivial to the serious, and I devoured these as well as many in the school library. I read the African Writers Series. I read Chinua Achebe, James Baldwin, Richard Wright, Maya Angelou, Alex Haley, Ayi Kwei Armah, Agatha Christie and Louis L'Amour, and I read the Hardy Boys books, Nancy Drew books and comic books like Hotshot Hamish, Archie and Veronica, Roy of the Rovers, Dennis the Menace, Superman and Beano. I read short stories in *Reader's Digest* and fairy tales in the Disney Book Club series of books.

Funny thing is, for all the reading I did, my father's biggest concern was that I read too much fiction. He wanted me to spend time on non-fiction. There I was thinking that the fact that I read voraciously would be enough. I have made up for it in more recent years, at least.

Perhaps what we need more of in the world is examples. Role models have always felt hollow or, possibly, it is because of who we hold up as role models. They are not perfect in the same way that none of us are. Sometimes it is hard to get beyond those imperfections.

I have always been grateful in that my form of 'hero worship' has never been wholehearted. That partly comes from a speech Malcolm X once gave where he said, to paraphrase, 'Don't take my words as law or absolute. Rather take them in, digest them, discard what doesn't make sense for you and take what works for you.' It was my first lesson in being discerning. It was also how I was raised to see everyone as flawed or great but equal. It doesn't matter who you are, at some stage you have to sit on the toilet, at some stage, hopefully once a day, you have bowel movements.

This outlook is also what helped me make sense of Spike Lee's *Jungle Fever*, which is about an interracial relationship. There is a scene in the movie where Wesley Snipes's character is ranting about children born of interracial unions that was in direct conflict with my being, considering I am the product of such a relationship. I still watch and love Wesley Snipes films. Plus, he made the *Malcolm X* movie.

I look at my son's and daughter's walls and wonder who will serve as heroes for them to put up. Will they even put up posters or will it just be home screen, profile or avatar pictures on a phone or tablet? They are growing up in a different time and I have reached the age where it feels like there is a dearth of people who inspire, so, regardless of who they post and place on the wall, I will probably disapprove. I find myself repeating my father's words when it comes to the music they listen to. He used to call mine 'boom-boom' music and I can't look past the crassness and shallowness of some of what they call music.

I look at who society exalts and feel they fall short of my heroes, plus they often seem extremely fallible to me. Or perhaps it is because I am becoming the 'old guy' who does not see beyond my ageist prejudices. My heroes have guided my life in a multitude of ways, often subtly, sometimes overtly.

In his book *Quantum Warrior*, John Kehoe talks of finding and talking to mentors, dead or alive, on an energy level. This means connecting with a part of their lives that speaks to you, and that you seek to learn from, and then connecting with that energy. I reckon, in a way, that is what I have done with my heroes. It isn't about everything they do but the parts that resonate with me.

I really hope my children will find theirs.

Our heroes

our heroes may be flawed
like we all are
but
our heroes
they remain
for their sacrifice
for the life they live
for the hope they birth in us
for the path they carve
for the example

For the love of music

I HAVE loved music for as long as I can remember. My father had a vinyl record collection that he regularly added to on his travels around the world. I now own that collection and there are few things that give me as much joy as listening to the soundtrack of my childhood, whether it is through a record player or streaming.

My father also used to collect Reader's Digest record packs, like rock of the fifties and sixties or jazz from the twenties to the seventies. In-between that, there was Miriam Makeba, Kori Moraba, Hugh Masekela, The Ramblers and Fela Kuti. As I grew older, I got into the music of my time, my era. In the early eighties, we started receiving cassette tapes from friends overseas with this thing called hip hop and it connected with my spirit in a way that was unexplained, even though it spoke of places and lives very different from mine. I loved pop music that came out of the UK, like Culture Club, Billy Idol, David Bowie and Wham.

Stevie Wonder is quoted as saying, 'Music, at its essence, is what gives us memories. And the longer a song has existed in our lives, the more memories we have of it.' We do create an endless soundtrack to our lives that can go into the millions for those of us who listen constantly. If you listened to ten songs a day, you would have listened to 25 550 individual songs in a year. Many of these songs weave themselves into our experiences, serving as reminders of emotions, moments and memories, as Stevie Wonder said.

I could tell you the songs that represent my first kiss – Sipho 'Hotstix' Mabuse's 'Burnout'; a car accident – Boyz II Men's 'End of the Road'; hot, summer Christmases in Maseru – no, not Boney M but Nat King Cole singing 'O Tannenbaum' (a favourite of my father's); and many other moments and the people who were part of those moments.

There are the many road trips we would take where I would play my music for my father in the hope that something would resonate. The one album he eventually loved was D'Angelo's *Brown Sugar*. I probably bought him at least four copies because my siblings would make them disappear.

Maxwell's *Urban Hang Suite* reminds me of driving to Grahamstown, where my brother Kweku and sister Efua went to boarding school. Toni Braxton's *Secrets* reminds of driving to East London one Christmas holiday. Mint Condition's *From the Mint Factory* reminds me of driving back from Durban after I had the operation on my leg. Mariah Carey's song 'Hero' helped me through the two weeks in hospital and still makes me a little teary.

In his book, *Mo' Meta Blues*, musician, producer and drummer for the group The Roots, Ahmir 'Questlove' Thompson, shares the journey of his life using the songs that were critical in his development, not just as a musician but as a human being. Reading the book resonated so much with me because, while not a musician, music is so intricately woven into my life.

And then there are the musicians I seem to connect with at a deeper level. I was eleven when Michael Jackson's *Thriller* came out and, yet, when I discovered Prince's music with the album *Purple Rain*, I became a life-long and obsessive fan. I was sad when Michael Jackson died. I shed a young tear when Prince died. I owned *Purple Rain* on cassette and still have the DVD and VHS video of the movie as well as the record. I have three books on Prince and have often gone down the Prince rabbit hole online.

I like a lot of artists, but then there are those whose music I will buy without even listening to it, well, at least in the pre-digital, pre-streaming days. It includes musicians like Massive Attack, Lenny Kravitz, Tricky, Meshell Ndegeocello, Outkast, Kamasi Washington, Public Enemy and Gregory Porter.

I often wonder why this is. What it is about them? Is it because there is an ambiguity in them and their music that perhaps only I see? Is it because they live outside of the boundaries of the boxes that society or industry likes to place around music? Whatever it is, they often hold exalted positions in my life's soundtrack for their artistry, their craft, as opposed to what they wear or who they hang out with. Their music is infused with their spirit, their energy, so perhaps that has something to do with it.

The list is longer than this and I keep adding to it, but I go back to them all regularly, either submerging myself in the past or creating new memories and new moments. Nostalgia has a wonderful way of papering over the cracks, allowing us to remember the good times. That can't be a bad thing.

Lean on me

IT WAS a Saturday afternoon. The concrete driveway sloped down for about 15 metres at an angle, ending with a black metal gate. Beside the driveway was a flat, square lawn of about 10 metres by 10 metres with budding trees and a disjointed hedge. A group of about fifteen young men in their early twenties were either sitting on the low wall running along the driveway or leaning up against cars, with hip hop playing out of one of them. The young men came from different families but had all grown up together, going to the same schools, partying in the same places, sometimes even liking the same girls.

I was one of these young men. We had gone from riding our bicycles and playing marbles through puberty to young men starting to come to terms with the responsibility of adulthood. Small cities are fertile breeding grounds for factions, with turf defined by how many in your crew watch your back when partying in spaces with other crews. You are forced into the same places as those on opposing sides because the city is so small.

Within those collectives, there are always those who are closer, those you define as your 'best friend', while you are still at an age where that language has a place. As you grow older, you start to drift apart. It is a funny thing when you have spent your entire life up to that point with a group of people and suddenly you find that the bond is fraying, without episode or conflict. One day, you wake up, and your best friend is no longer your best friend and someone you had a distant relationship with is, just like that, the person you spend most of your time with. Coming to terms with that is part of growing up, I guess. That and realising that there is nothing wrong with it.

Some friendships are proper break-ups, bringing with them conflict and tension, usually when the things that you were able to gloss over become deal-breakers. Yet, all of a sudden, you are ten years older and realise that that is also part of growing up and often what was said or done really doesn't matter much in the general scheme of things. I have had a lot of such moments over the years.

I watched my father, after getting divorced from my younger brothers' and sister's mother, go from having a social life as part of a group of friends and family to spending his nights alone at home, when he wasn't working. And he always seemed to be working. When I was in my twenties, and we were the only two living in the house, he would ask me to chill at home with him on weekends, but I was too busy running the streets to even take a moment to realise that he was, at times, lonely.

We lived together and worked together. Last thing I wanted, at the time, was to spend the free time I had with Daddy, talking. There were parties to go to and girls to chat up and drinks to be drunk, often excessively. And, with hindsight, I do reckon I could have accommodated him more, but, at the same time, I was going through the journey of coming into my own.

Ironically, as I have grown older, I have become more like him, despite having a wife and children to fill my time at home with conversation and activity. I have also had the opportunity to reflect on friendships, particularly as a boy and a man. I know a lot of people, yet, when it comes down to it, I have gone through life with a handful of true friendships, of best friends. There have been, perhaps, two handfuls of other boys/men who have held a position in my life that goes beyond hanging out when socially convenient. These are people who were so ingrained in my life, who have known my doubts and inadequacies and fears in a way that very few have or will.

These are people who, for an extended period, I could call on or could call on me, regardless of the circumstances. And they have remained a part of my life, although we are not in each other's lives as much as we used to be. I often wonder how that works. How two individuals go from strangers to brothers. How you go from perhaps bumping into each other on occasion to confidantes. Today, as I write this, it has been exactly a year since my friend, my business partner, my 'brother' Gerrard passed away suddenly.

For a couple of years, we orbited each other without actually meeting. We knew the same people, had spent time in the same places and even worked on the same projects. My first concrete memory of him was at a meeting around 2007 to talk about a project I was working on with my cousin's TV production company and he was managing an artist. From there, we started to cross paths more often and then, one day, I looked up and we were business partners, and friends, and brothers. We talked every day, sometimes several times a day. We propped each other up. We were there for each other, always. And then he was gone.

Our standard line was 'it is what it is' whenever faced with life's daily struggles, but, on the day that he transitioned, it became hollow. He was 38 years old. He was the person who, if anything happened to me and Estelle, would be responsible for raising my children with the same values that I try to raise them with. And then he was gone.

His death hit me harder than that of my father's. It feels weird to say that out loud, but my father had lived a full life. As the cliché goes, he had fought the good fight and it was time for him to rest. Whatever that means. Gerrard was in a good place, full of energy, full of plans. After some years of fluctuating fortunes, things were starting to turn around and he was driving that process, for both of us, and his mother, Charlene, as well as his brother, Dexter.

Death is most difficult for the living. For the religious, there are the usual 'he's in a better place', 'the Lord has a plan for all of us', etc. When you are not that way inclined, it becomes harder to find consolation or the semblance of peace and acceptance. And yet, you have to learn how to accept things to be able to continue the job of living.

The hardest lesson for me has been learning how to keep my own counsel. Gerrard and my father were the two people I used to 'run things by' as I tried to make sense of life. In the span of two short years, they were both gone, and since then everything stays in my head. The different considerations when making a decision about work or life or parenting; the different songs or sneakers or dope designs that I come across that I want to share with the one person who gets it. In an instant, I can't tell somebody.

I often sit and wonder whether there will ever be someone to fill that gap. Death creates a void. It creates a hole in our lives that was occupied by a specific and unique person. We all have people around us who love us and care for us and will serve as the shoulders we lean on, but they can never be that specific person.

For months after Gerrard passed away, I would wonder whether I would find another 'best friend'. If my personal history is anything to go by, I don't know. I have friends but none who are as close as he was. Yet, I also recognise that friendships of this nature cannot be planned. They cannot be forced. I have my brothers who were once at the centre of my universe and, although they are still with us in this physical realm, they now reside on the edges. And that's all right. Adulthood can be complicated and difficult, but the living have to keep on living until it is their ... our ... my ... time to go.

Dining-room table

IT'S AMAZING how you can interact with an object countless times and then one day, suddenly, a seemingly random thought pops into your mind. I am sitting at the dining-room table, alone. It is a dark wood table with lighter streaks running along it, barely discernible but there all the same. The chair that I am sitting on is part of a set that didn't come with the table. Those were dark wood as well with tan cushions. They were finally replaced a few years beyond their sitting-on date. The chairs were wobbly, the fabric on the cushion fraying; sitting on them was often an act of trust and faith that they wouldn't collapse underneath you.

My father bought the dining-room table when we moved into our first townhouse, three years after we got married. Before that we lived in a two-bedroom apartment that didn't have room for dining anywhere, just space for the small lounge suite my mother-in-law, Elaine, bought for us as a wedding gift. My father was visiting for the weekend not long after we moved into our spot and went out on a Saturday morning with Estelle. He also bought us our first DStv decoder on that outing.

More than fifteen years later, we still have the dining-room table. We have moved twice with it, spending three years in one house, eight in the next and four years in the house we are living in. My mother-in-law is no longer with us. Neither is my father and the dining-room table is the only piece of furniture that they both experienced. We don't sit at it regularly, but today, for some reason, I can't get over how, in its own strange way, it reminds me of my father, and not because he bought it.

My father was big on sitting at the table for dinner. It probably came from the time he lived in Germany. I am speculating. In my time in Germany after high school, I moved three times to a different family within my year there and the one common denominator amongst all my families was that we sat together for breakfast, lunch and supper every day.

Until my early teens, it was often my job to set the table: the placement of the different forks and knives, the soup and dessert spoon, place mats for the plates and various dishes that housed the food for that particular meal. We never prayed. I grew up in a house where you decided what route you wanted to take spiritually. Although a preacher of sorts when he moved to Germany for an apprenticeship in his mid-twenties, my father had 'lost his faith' as an African living in Europe during the sixties and seventies.

As his marriage to my younger siblings' mother deteriorated, we spent less time eating at the table. Also, the challenges of running his own business and raising five children made it harder for him to be home for meals at the table. Supper was eaten on the couch in front of the television.

In later years, when I had long moved out of the house, and the country, we would have dinner at the table whenever we visited. It was always a great opportunity to catch up and enjoy each other's company.

My random thought? The dining-room table is more than a piece of furniture. It is a gathering place for families and friends. It is a place where we can take a moment from the busyness of life to catch up, get to know each other and just be. Food has a way of creating community and the dining-room table represents the coming together for food and nourishment physically, mentally and, dare I say, spiritually. Even the rituals around sitting at the table together are lessons. You don't just leave the table when you have finished eating; if you need to get up, you ask to be excused. It is a moment to be present in the company of those dear to you. While we may not do it daily as a family, the moments when we do are always priceless.

Listen to your footsteps

SOMETIMES THE lessons come from the unlikeliest of places. You hear something. Or see something. And days, weeks, months or years later, the proverbial penny drops. My sprint coach in Oldenburg, Germany, was an old man with a face marked with a maze of red veins and a tentative walk. He had fought in World War II, been captured and somehow ended up in Canada for a period. I never could make sense of the timeline, but that's what he told me. His English was spotty and my German non-existent when he recounted his experiences as a prisoner of war. My German got better, but we never returned to his war stories, so I work with what my erratic memory serves up.

Having become a sprinter, specialising in 100 metres while in high school, the first thing I did when I arrived in Germany was to find an athletics club. It did help that I carried a German passport at the time and could, therefore, run in the district and national championships. I did the former but left before I could try for the latter.

My first six months in Germany were spent learning and perfecting technique. In Maseru, I had primarily trained myself from the time I discovered I was relatively fast. I don't know what it is that drew me to sprinting in a school that was a bit of an island; we never competed against other schools in the country. I do know that there are few greater feelings than looking down the track, focusing in on your lane, tuning everything else out, except the starter. This was even so on our school track, which was grass, with clay patches and lonely tufts of grass creating tiny hurdles in-between. I ran barefoot for years and sprained my ankle regularly, so I needed to strap my ankles up when I ran.

Once a year, we had our sports day where the whole school would turn out to either watch or participate, with no classes happening on the day. I was one of the fastest in school for at least four years in a row. I think I won twice and broke the school record once, but it was broken again not long after that, so I didn't have that record for long.

To prepare for sports day, I would watch my PE teacher's training videos by British decathlon athlete Daley Thompson and train after school. The running, very cheesy joke amongst my high-school friends was that, every day, I ran against myself ... and lost.

During school holidays, I would make the fifteen-minute walk every morning from home to Setsoto Stadium, where a group of soldiers trained every morning. From my understanding, soldiers who showed athletic ability were part of this programme, which meant that, while their fellow soldiers were doing whatever soldiers do on a daily basis, they simply needed to run. There was no formal coach and the main sergeant used to lead us in training. It was often brutal, with one's insides left on the side of the track on a good day.

While training in Oldenburg, my coach would go on about the importance of listening to your footsteps when you ran. He trained us to use the sound to gauge how quickly we were moving our feet. At the start, out of the blocks, footsteps are closer together and, as you straighten up, your strides lengthen, meaning your footsteps are further apart. I can still hear him going 'ta, ta, ta..ta..ta...ta....ta' as he drummed the concept into our heads.

I carried that with me through to university in Durban, where I was trying to qualify to run for Lesotho at the 1996 Summer Olympics in Atlanta. I had it all worked out. At 24 in 1996, I would make the final eight and, hopefully, win a medal. Between 1996 and the 2000 Olympics, I would then be doing the international athletics meet circuit, including world championships, and win. By 28, in 2000, I would win the gold medal.

Everything was going according to plan until, in my last year of university, the aftermath of a particularly hard basketball game ended any hopes I had of running again. Through high school and at university, I would experience stiffness with a dull, aching pain in the tibialis anterior muscles (basically the muscle opposite the calf, next to the shin) in both my legs. A short break from any strenuous activity would ease the pain and I would be able to continue afterwards.

In this game, on a Saturday evening in June 1994, I powered through the pain; as a result, it didn't subside and became progressively worse. Back in my room on campus, I took multiple painkillers, which did not help. At some stage, I was banging my head on the wall to distract from the pain. I crawled to the res sub-warden's room for him to call the residence doctor, but he never arrived.

The following morning, I was able to get a friend to drive me to the local hospital, King Edward VII Hospital, where I sat for an hour or two amidst the aftermath of a Saturday night – stab wounds and the like. The doctor who saw me took at X-ray, told me it was a muscle strain and sent me on my way with more painkillers. That evening, the res doctor eventually emerged, said the same thing, and left me with even more painkillers and sleeping pills.

On Monday morning, since I was struggling to walk, I went to another hospital to rent crutches. On Tuesday morning, I decided to see the doctor on campus. He looked at me for five minutes and immediately called a specialist at another hospital and sent me there. At the mercy of friends with cars, I was eventually able to get to the specialist, who also examined me for five minutes and declared that I needed an operation, but he wasn't available. He then called another specialist and told me to go there.

I have always felt uneasy in hospitals. This is possibly the aftermath of ending up in hospital after the car accident. Fortunately, I had some coins on me and called my father in Lesotho from the payphone to let him know what was going on. The friend who dropped me off found me sitting on the curb, close to tears. He drove me to the next doctor, who immediately directed me to the hospital to be admitted. We rushed back to my res for clothes and toiletries and my friend dropped me off.

This was the only time in my life I ever swore at my father. We had been going through financial difficulties and, when I got to the hospital, he was on the phone with the head of finance who would not allow me to be admitted without a deposit of R5 000. She and my father were going back and forth until I grabbed the phone and basically told my father to stop fucking around. I had burst a blood vessel in my leg and as the blood leaked, filling up my leg from my foot upwards, the pain was excruciating as the muscle basically rotted in my leg. That will forever be my excuse.

Within an hour, I was in theatre where the anaesthetist fumbled first with finding a vein – I told her at the rate she was going, they wouldn't need to anaesthetise – and then she hit the light switch instead of whatever switch she was supposed to be flicking.

I woke up to a dark room that wasn't my bedroom. I couldn't feel my leg. In a panic, I threw off the blankets and, to my relief, saw my toes were still there. And then the pain hit. The only instruction that had lodged itself in my mind, after I came out of theatre, was when in pain, press red button. Morphine is a wonderful drug but not good for you in the long run. It was my friend during that period.

I was to go into theatre two more times. The first time, the surgeon Mr Mills simply sliced into my leg, leaving a 30-centimetre cut to allow the blood to leak out. The second time, he cut out my muscle. The third time, he stitched me up.

I kept asking whether I would be able to run again, but he could only bring himself to tell me 'no' after a week in hospital. I spent two weeks in hospital and over three months on crutches. I was declared 30 per cent permanently disabled by Mr Mills. I navigated mid-year exams for my final year on sleeping pills and painkillers. I missed two exams, which I had to write later in the year. I wore a custom-made prosthetic support because my foot drooped; I couldn't lift it up. I eventually had three supports, two of which I designed myself for greater movement at the ankle. Without the support, I couldn't drive and my foot would slap down when I walked.

We heard about a muscle transfer procedure that could make walking easier. But it could only be done in the US. My father had friends he had worked with on a Lesotho project based in Tucson, Arizona. We went back and forth on the possibility of my travelling there to have the operation done. It would have been costly, and I would have to stay in the US for at least a month for recovery. We eventually decided against it.

There were no orthopaedic surgeons in Lesotho. For patients who needed those specialists, they would be put on a list for when there were visiting surgeons, which used to happen once or twice a year, with surgeons coming primarily from India and Belgium. I wasn't on the list, but a friend was able to get me in when a group of Belgian surgeons came in 1996. I had to decide whether to go ahead with it or not because the surgeon who examined me put the chances of success at 60 per cent. He also said that, over time, the muscles would become weaker, even if the op was successful.

My father was out of the country, but, fortunately, our offices were across the road from the hospital so I ran the businesses from hospital for about a week. The mechanics of the operation involved splitting the tendon from a small muscle on the inside of my leg, just above the ankle, and attaching one half to the top of my foot to help me pull my foot up. There are few feelings as traumatic as trying to move a part of your body and it doesn't. I can't begin to imagine what it is like to be fully paralysed. The operation was relatively successful in that it enabled me to walk without support.

There are a couple of key lessons that I have learned from this process. The first is that hurting my leg saved me the unenviable task of, as the cliché goes, putting my money where my mouth is. It's all just theory now. I don't have to worry about proving it – the winning gold medals thing. Fortunately, I don't dwell on the what-ifs. I have also learned how to move on quite well, regardless of the situation. I have found that dwelling on things for too long can be counter-productive. I do tend to overthink situations and scenarios, but there's always the moment when I decide 'f*** it' and move on to something else.

That is how I left the family businesses and moved to Joburg. It's how I left a TV production company in 2008, telling them on a Wednesday that I wasn't signing the contract for a new production so my last day would be that Friday. When I worked for *Blaque* magazine, I sent a resignation email on Sunday afternoon, went in on Monday to collect my stuff and went to the mall with my then two-year-old son. With *Destiny Man*, although it was a drawn-out resignation process, a week after I left, I was asked if I missed it, and I hadn't thought about it for the whole week. I was focused on what I was going to be doing moving forward.

I also learned that it is important to have options, especially for athletes. If I didn't have the options, who knows where I would have ended up. Plus, in a way, not having running meant that I explored other skills; would I have ended up doing poetry, or getting involved in fashion, or IT or the media?

I am forced to reflect on this regularly because, to this day, I can't help but listen to my footsteps when I walk. When I wore my support, it made an inconsistent plonk when I walked. Before the muscle transfer operation, my foot would slap on the ground. Even with the transfer, I have a slight limp – although I have turned it into a swagger of sorts – and I took to walking on the ball of my right foot when at home, which I still do, unconsciously. I have 'bad leg' days when the sound of my footsteps irritates me. Inconsistent. Erratic. My limp is more pronounced when I am tired. Sometimes I trip over my toes when I'm not concentrating.

And yet, listening to my footsteps has helped me navigate life across the board. Sometimes I need to concentrate on my footsteps, which needs me to be present. And being present in life needs me to reflect on what I am doing while I am doing it. It's a weird form of mindfulness borne out of trauma. There's always a silver lining.

Books, books, books

TO AVOID writing by reading seems a strange thing to do. Or not. Too often I read the words of others and conclude that, perhaps, the world is better suited to having their words than mine. You are reading this so, fortunately, for me at least, that conclusion is a temporary one.

Reading is a two-way conversation between writer and reader. It is the reader who gives the words meaning and life and, sometimes, when reading something, I have an internal conversation with the author, wanting to put into words what I would say to them if we met. And then I don't write anything but simply shift on to the next page.

Until this page.

Neil Gaiman, one of my favourite writers, reflects in his book *The View from the Cheap Seats* on libraries, bookshops and the books that shaped him. His reflections had me reflecting on the role that books – and places that house books – have had on my life, starting with home.

My father, having been an academic, converted the garage in our new home into his study when I was eleven. In the years before that, he had a typical study in the National University of Lesotho-owned house that we lived in while he was still lecturing. The original study had an oak table, a leather work chair and shelves on one side of the room, filled with books. He had books on every subject conceivable and, for his whole life, he continued to add to that. In my younger years, I gravitated towards the fiction books, of which there were few. He remained a fervent believer in reading for knowledge and I don't remember seeing him actually read a novel.

He must have, at some stage, because we had an impressive collection of the African Writers Series, with novels by the likes of Can Themba, Alex La Guma, Chinua Achebe, Ngũgĩ wa Thiong'o, Ayi Kwei Armah, Bessie Head and Wole Soyinka.

I started with the Hardy Boys and Nancy Drew, which I borrowed from our neighbours, moving onto the African Writers Series from about ten years old. I do remember going to the National Library in Maseru regularly but very little of what I read from there. My father subscribed to the *Reader's Digest* and, from them, I would get thick, hardcover volumes of fairy tales.

The library that was defining was my high-school library. The librarian was a tall, American woman, Mrs Fritsch, whose two sons were also at my school. I went through a big Louis L'Amour phase and he seemed to put out a book every other month, telling the stories of various American Western families, the gunfights and the feuds. For some reason, Westerns appealed to me. South Africa's TV4 channel used to play a Western, invariably with John Wayne, every Friday and I built an extensive Betamax video collection of these.

This was before I came to understand the politics of the American West and how Black people and Native Americans/First Nation people were portrayed and treated. But this was much later in my life. Whenever a new Louis L'Amour book arrived in the library, Mrs Fritsch would make sure that I got my hands on it before anyone else. This was probably the start of a habit I have when it comes to reading. I get into particular authors, devour all their books as quickly as I can and then spend years lamenting their writing output, while they work on their next book. I remember waiting for eons for Robert Jordan's next book in the Wheel of Time series, only to discover that he had passed away.

It still bothers me, although I now understand how hard writing a book actually is. It was always better with older writers like Agatha Christie and the Sherlock Holmes series of stories because they had written all they were going to write.

Another library that will always have a special place in my heart is a foreign-language library in Oldenburg. I sometimes wonder whether it is still there and what it looks like. I had exhausted the library at the university in town, which only had a couple of shelves of books in English, when I discovered it existed. I would make the 30-minute bicycle ride every few weeks; Oldenburg was a bicycle town with pavements divided into pedestrian and bicycle lanes and a bicycle image on the traffic lights.

The building wasn't much to write home about. It was a rectangular building, with brick walls (I think), not that big, but big enough to house enough books to satisfy my needs. Funnily enough, I would read the back cover of the same books constantly, before taking one or two out. I reckon there are books I looked at over ten times before something about them caught my fancy. I still do that.

It was here that I discovered Joseph Heller's *Catch-22*. There are books that you can't get enough of, and this is one of those for me. I couldn't tell you why. I probably read it about five times in that year and have reread it countless times since. It is also one of the few books that I have read that was turned into a film/TV series that I also enjoyed.

I read Henry Miller's *Tropic of Capricorn* and *Tropic of Cancer* several times, but, I suspect, being a nineteen-year-old, the explicitness of the books appealed to me. I haven't read them since.

That library in Germany is probably the last library I frequented. I don't even remember whether the library at my university in Durban had fiction. It was the place I went to read thick, sometimes dreary, books on Economics and the like when I was studying. I got novels from friends and then, later, from bookshops when I could afford them.

With the advent of Amazon, I initially started ordering books and, after buying myself a Kindle, I switched to digital books. Most recently, I have switched back to physical books and order most of them online, with the occasional visit to a bookshop.

My home bookshelves are starting to look like my father's. Plus, there are some of his books on my shelves. When he passed away, all I could think was, how do I save the books?

A part of me hopes my children with have the same dilemma. A part of me is just grateful for the opportunity to escape into other worlds, although, ironically, I now read more non-fiction than fiction. I suspect my father is pleased.

Escape

THE RUSSIAN author Fyodor Dostoevsky is quoted as having said, 'To think too much is a disease.' I have always wondered how one measures thinking too much. I have spent a lifetime in my head and been told I think too much. I have always felt that, in some instances, we don't think enough and what children should be taught is how to think. So many things in the world seem to happen because zero thought has been put into a situation and the consequences of this lack of thought creates conflict, on different scales.

But I have also come to recognise that to live primarily in one's head is not conducive to, well, living in harmony with others. It can be a crutch, this retreat into one's self. It leaves very little room for anything else, especially when you define yourself as solely your mind. Learning that I am not my mind has been a complicated exercise that I am still working through.

For a long time, if my mind wasn't working constantly, I would struggle to sleep. Now, when my mind is racing, unpacking scenarios, making plans, stressing about the world's challenges, I struggle to sleep.

My father brought a television into the house around 1982. Prior to this, I had submerged myself in the written world, but this was a whole new world. While what one could watch was limited, all of a sudden we didn't have to go to the cinema, which was rare in itself, to escape. The only channels available were from South Africa, primarily in English and Afrikaans, with a spattering of programming in Setswana, isiZulu and isiXhosa. A lack of understanding of some of the languages didn't stop me from planting myself on the floor in front of the telly and zoning out.

Looking back, it occurs to me that the things that I fell into deeply involved a temporary escape from reality. It is only when reading a book or watching a movie or television programme that my mind settles. Being transported into another world or other lives is the only time I am not stressing, plotting, thinking and worrying. When I was younger, I used to do this regularly, but, as I became an adult, I stopped doing it as much, which has resulted in overthinking and being constantly wired too tightly.

The irony today is that we have so many things that serve as a distraction but bring with them added stress. Social media is not an escape but a magnifying glass on the challenges of the world. We have so many opportunities to watch films and series that the excessive number of options make it even harder to choose what to engage with.

Having children reduced the time available to spend on video, at a time when I probably need to be a lot more deliberate about taking time for myself, away from adulting, away from being a father, husband, brother, friend, professional, etc. Added to this is the reality that most of my work is 'head work' and the majority of my reading over the last decade has been non-fiction, so I am constantly thinking and processing.

It has got to the stage where I can't watch 'intelligent' films that make you think because I find them tiring. Now I just want to watch good old-fashioned action flicks with the usual story lines.

We need to be able to escape. We need to be able to step away from life and its complexities. I used to have hobbies. As I write this, I realise I need to find or rather make the space for them.

A life of crime

THE NEIGHBOURHOOD I grew up in, called Lower Florida, from aged five to eleven, was typical of Maseru. We were, to all intents and purposes, an upper middle-class family, by Lesotho's standards, with my father a lecturer, and my siblings' mother in the legal profession and later working for a bank. We lived in a National University of Lesotho house, surrounded by families of different economic standing. Some of my friends would have to herd sheep after school.

We would all play together on the dusty, dirt road that lead to our homes, riding our bicycles, playing football, making and driving wire cars and playing with marbles – we had a marble football pitch in my neighbour's front yard, with batteries serving as the goalposts. Because our neighbourhood was on the edge of the Mohokare (Caledon) River, which is the border between South Africa and Lesotho, we would go down to the riverbanks and play there. Sometimes we would appropriate maize from the farm just across the river and roast our takings over a fire, ruining our appetites for supper that night.

We also had a small bicycle track with humps to launch our bicycles off. It had been built by some guys who would come and ride their motorcycles there occasionally, but it was in our neighbourhood, so it was ours.

Another thing we used to do with the kids from Upper Florida was shoplift. There was no real morality to it. Usually, during school holidays, we would get together before we headed out, and then reconvene to show our pickings. I had a beautiful beige bomber jacket I got in Germany and I had cut slits on the inside to enable me to slip whatever I wanted easily into the lining.

The other advantage I had was that, coming from a more well-to-do family, and having a bicycle, I could comfortably go to the town centre – Maseru only officially became a city in 1993 – and find goodies in the local supermarket, OK Bazaars, and the stationery shop, CNA. In my first year of high school, I did good business selling Staedler colouring pencils, which came in packs of 12 or 24, and were needed for school, especially geography and art class. I used to take ice cream from the ice-cream guy as payment – Choc Chip and Caramel Crunch were the most expensive, so I usually went for those.

Until, one day, I got caught. I was about ten/eleven years old. I had gone to OK one morning alone. I padlocked my bicycle to a lamp post outside and went in to see what I could get. I found a double-cassette album of Stevie Wonder's, which I slipped into the front of my shorts and pulled my T-shirt over. Just as a I got to the exit, the supermarket security stopped me. He tapped the cassettes and hauled me to a small storeroom in the back of the building, beyond those big rubber doors, which don't snap back fully when you walk through them, that every supermarket seems to have.

Initially, I didn't want to give him my name or my father's, but, after 30 minutes in that cold room, I gave up everything, including my father's phone number. He left me alone in the room and called my father, who took hours, or so it seemed, to arrive with a Ghanaian friend of his, Uncle Barry, who was a teacher at my high school.

After they let me go, all my father said was to ride my bike straight home, have a bath and wait for him, which I dutifully did. Sitting in my bedroom waiting for him was excruciating. He walked in, finally, told me to get my belt from the wardrobe, made me kneel over the edge of the bed and asked me to tell him everything I had ever stolen. I, foolishly, told the whole truth, going through a long shopping list of items, to be interrupted, halfway through my confession, with the first strike of the belt. At first, it was easy to take, then he found his range, hitting the same strip of my little butt repeatedly.

I have always wondered where he learned how to wield a belt so well because he didn't believe in hitting us and that was the first time I had ever been hit with a belt. I never did get to ask him.

After this experience and the lecture that accompanied it, my life of crime was over, until university. At university, being an Economics student, and things being difficult at home financially, I needed books so I started buying from a guy who used to steal them for me. After about six months of our first year, he, inconveniently, was excluded due to poor academic performance. I decided to become my own supplier, relieving the local bookshop of the books I needed for class. A couple of friends, discovering this, asked me to get them a few books and, before I knew it, I was stealing books for pocket money.

At the start of my third and last year, it occurred to me that throwing all the hard work away just for some textbooks did not make sense and I officially retired from shoplifting.

In-between this, a high-school friend of mine from Joburg had wandered far off the beaten path and was stealing cars and peddling drugs, mandrax, in particular. He convinced some of us to find him buyers and to find cars for him.

I tried one deal with a friend in Durban and met a buyer in Lesotho, but it fell through. A few months later, driving through Maseru while on holiday from varsity, I drove past an unmarked car that was known to belong to the police and saw the prospective buyer sitting comfortably in the passenger seat.

That was my true moment of clarity. Firstly, I am not, by nature, a dishonest person and all that this foolishness would do is get me into unnecessary trouble. Secondly, I had too much going for me. I was fortunate in ways that some of my friends weren't. The messages from the universe were loud and clear, and, if I didn't heed them, the next message would potentially be the loudest and the most painful.

So, I walked away. Sometimes I wonder where I would be if I hadn't heeded the messages. There have been multiple moments in my life like that when something pulls me from the brink. I have learned to listen and act accordingly.

The drugs made me do it

THE NIGHT before was a blur, but the day after does not make sense unless you look at the day before. There was a new club opening in Randburg, Johannesburg, called Cream. I was to meet up with three friends there that night and I had been looking forward to this Saturday night, but I first had to make it through the day and my Aunt Pam.

My first two years in Joburg had not gone as planned so, after a short stint living in my own townhouse in Bryanston, I had moved in with her. I was running my own business, an IT consulting company called Baffoe Kakana (BAKA) Consulting in partnership with a friend. Although I was often broke, somehow I always seemed to have money for drugs – primarily ecstasy and cocaine, with a little acid when budget and/or friends allowed. I am using the word 'friends' loosely. They were people I used to drug with, and, in truth, that was what brought us together, as opposed to any type of connection or commonality of spirit, interests and the like.

It is a bit of a journey to that point, follow me. In Maseru, there was word that some of the guys were doing cocaine, but, in general, we smoked a bit of weed and drank copiously. That was the extent of my exposure to any type of mind-altering substance. As an athlete, I only drank occasionally through high school and, while I drank a bit more at university, I would pay for it on the track and in the gym daily.

There was a period after university when I was a borderline alcoholic, needing to pick up a bottle or two of cider on my drive home from work, just to stop my hands from trembling a bit. At my worst, I would stop over at my neighbourhood tavern for a couple of drafts of beer each day after work. If not that, then on Wednesday evenings we would buy a case of ciders and a bottle of cheap whiskey and head out to the National University of Lesotho for some midweek partying.

Weed? That came after my operations and the abrupt end of my sprinting career. It got to the point where I was usually passed out in the car outside whichever party I was at because weed and alcohol combined rendered me senseless. Chicco, who I was always with, would handle the drive to drop off whoever was with us, and then drop himself off. All I had to do was be conscious enough to drive myself home from his home – fortunately, it was not too long a drive – and climb into bed, without waking up my father. I do suspect he heard me every time.

When I moved up to Joburg, it was more of the same until, one day, heading out to a rave and needing something a little stronger, I was given half a white pill, which I was told to chew and swallow. It was bitter, the kind of taste that makes you shudder, but, on that day, I was only interested in getting high. I had smoked and drunk at a braai, which, coupled with a disagreement with the person I was seeing at the time, had me feeling sober and in need of something to dull the emotions. I was looking for a distraction. The white pill was an ecstasy pill and, rather than softening the edges, it put me on a high that I had never experienced before.

It is said that we only use a certain percentage of our brains. In this instance, I discovered that we only use a small percentage of our senses because they all seemed to be ramped up, operating at superhuman levels. Throw in a rave with thousands of people, pounding music and light waves that seemed to penetrate your fingers when you put your hands up, and I had found my thing.

I have always been a little shy and introverted. I was never comfortable in new spaces or around new people. I liked my world and my navigation through it to be a certain way and, if it deviated, I would withdraw. It was something that was always remarked on when friends and family were encouraging me to be more outgoing. Society seemed to say, when you are introverted, there is something wrong with you. On ecstasy, I was the person the world around me said I should be. I would wander around raves, striking up conversations, making friends and generally being the outgoing person I was supposed to be, or so I thought.

This became my life, at least from Thursday to Saturday. I was focused from Monday to Thursday, before night fell. Come Thursday night, I would be dropping my first pill at a club in Rosebank called Foundations. Friday, after a couple of hours of sleep, it was off to Sandton for my standing appointment with my barber. I would always have pancakes at Walnut Grove, read a music magazine, get some groceries and then head to the office for a couple of hours. Drinks in Sandton in the late afternoon … hit the clubs, rinse and repeat. Sundays were my day to chill. My then girlfriend was a flight attendant and was usually working international flights, generally arriving home late Saturdays or Sunday mornings, so on Sundays we caught up.

This particular Saturday, the Saturday I was supposed to be meeting friends at the launch of Cream, she was in town. My cousin was in a Church of Scientology rehab, undergoing what is called the Purification Rundown, and he was coming home for the weekend. Somehow, Aunt Pam hustled me into driving her to go and pick him up, which was just an excuse to reprimand me about my lifestyle. Some parents are oblivious to what their children get up to. She is not one of those. She made it a point to educate herself on all aspects of drug culture and rehab facilities. She could look at you once and determine what you were on. My cousin, who had been grappling for longer than I had, had finally decided to do something about it so I was under pressure to also change my ways.

We got to the centre, a house in Kensington, which was also the home of a woman with her two kids. Double storey with a big yard out back, it looked and felt more like a hippie commune than a centre for those looking to pull themselves back from the precipice. For an hour, I had two middle-aged women tag-teaming me, telling me I need to sort my shit out. The irony was that I had had a heavy one the night before and all I could think about was the acid I had in my pocket and the night ahead.

Finally, I got home and took a nap. As I was getting ready to head out, the girlfriend phoned to tell me her car had been stolen. I headed over to her place, commiserated for an hour or so and finally left for Foundations, because my people had left Cream. I dropped the acid in the car. I got an ecstasy pill from my dealer, ended up doing some lines of cocaine in the bathroom and hit the dance floor. My next memory is being led out of the club, without my spectacles. I wasn't in a state to drive so I was driven to a friend's place where I caught a couple of hours of sleep. When I got home, the shit was hitting the fan. I went to my girlfriend's place, hoping to get some recovery time. She told me to leave because she was not going to waste her time with a junkie. Nowhere to go, I ended up back at the rehab spot. That was the last time I did any type of drugs. It was a moment when the universe gave me two options – gutter or clean – and, fortunately, I chose the right one. Some of the people I was around didn't make it and ended up in the proverbial gutter.

Would I change the experience? I have the benefit of looking back and so I would say no, because I made it beyond and am here to tell the tale. There are those who went deeper, into harder drugs, and also found their way out. I made it through the Purification programme and came out the other side better for it. I came out with an improved understanding of myself, my inadequacies and my weaknesses. I came out with a clearer picture of my triggers and how I used substances of different sorts as crutches, as excuses for not dealing with life.

There have been people and spaces and experiences that make it easier for me to relapse and I cut those out of my life completely. And, while I did start drinking again a year after the end of rehab, I learned how to both drink for the enjoyment, as opposed to getting drunk, and how to say no when it isn't convenient for me. Plus, the older I am, the longer it takes to recover from a heavy night. I did start smoking weed again for a short while but haven't smoked in over twelve years now because it hasn't appealed to me. Will I do weed again? Who knows? It is legal in the home now. My joy is in cigars, smoking them, learning about the craft of making them, and the different types and flavours.

Cocaine? I have always contended that something that nice just can't be good for you. To try again would be to slip back down into the abyss. Life is too good and there's too much at stake for me to stand on the precipice again.

Looking back

AS TIME passes, the stains of the past feel a little less dark. Moments that seemed unsurmountable fade away, leaving you, hopefully, a little lighter, life a little brighter. As a teenager and as a young man, I often wallowed in the darkness. I struggled to see the forest for the trees, which I sometimes regret. As I grow older, I am able to look back and take the lessons from each experience.

After about two weeks in hospital following the operations on my leg, my closest friend at the time walked into my room in res to find me sitting on the edge of my bed, distraught, the tears dripping onto the running spikes on my feet. I don't think I will ever be able to put into words the feeling of willing my foot to move, and nothing happening. I loved sprinting. I loved how I felt at the start of a race, staring down the track, oblivious to everything but the lane between the two white lines. That moment, at varsity, was when I realised that I would never run again, not the way I used to, not even close to the way I used to.

The dream of running at the Olympics, which I had held close for more than ten years, was over, even before I had really begun. All the people who said it was a pipe dream had been proven right.

And yet, when I look at what my life has been since, chances are slim that I would have had the experiences I have had and been in the spaces I have been.

Losing my mother at such a young age drastically altered the trajectory of my life. There was a time when I used to sit and imagine what life would have been like if she had lived. And yet, I turned out all right – kinda – and have lived a full and rich life so far. I can't work with what-ifs and have learned to accept that it is what it is.

Losing a baby in our first year of marriage was painful. And the journey to try to get pregnant again tested both our relationship and us individually. I always wanted a family and I had to ask myself the very difficult question: if we couldn't have children, would I want to stay married? Fortunately, the honest answer was, and is, yes, and, while the pregnancy was difficult, and the aftermath even harder, I would like to think it brought us closer together. We went through fertility clinics, procedures and uncertainty together and have two wonderful children.

I left Lesotho at a time when my father needed me most to rebuild after political unrest in Lesotho resulted in our offices getting partially burned. I can comfortably admit that it was probably the greatest disappointment that I caused my father. And yet, the life I have been able to build and the people who have enriched me in amazing ways – Estelle, Kweku and Ayanna – would any of this have happened?

Every choice we make alters the trajectory of our lives. I learn every day from each one I make. And I live by the one-foot-in-front-of-the-other philosophy. When times are hard, all I do is keep putting one foot in front of the other and, eventually, when I look up, I have walked my way out of the darkness into the light.

When we are young, each trying moment feels like the end of the world. By the time you hit your forties, you realise that it isn't that deep. This is one of the biggest lessons I learned from watching my father live life. It was full, rich and filled with experiences that, I would like to think, made the hard times worth it. I know that it is the case for me. The road ahead is still, hopefully, long, but I have no real regrets when it comes to the past. Every moment has been a learning experience that has made me a better version of me. And every moment to come will continue to make me better, as long as I keep learning.

IDENTITY AND BELONGING

Daddy, what colour am I?

KWEKU MUST have been about three years old. It was a Sunday morning on a typical Johannesburg summer day. I'm not sure what time it was exactly, but the sun had just risen and it wasn't time for me to wake up. My son, sleeping in the bed between my wife and I, nudged me and said that he needed to go to the toilet for a number two.

Eyes half-shut, I took him to the bathroom, helped him sit on the toilet and perched on the edge of the bath, waiting for him to finish his business. He was chatty. I was trying to retain enough sleepiness to ensure that I could go back to sleep when he was done. You know, when you keep your eyes at half-mast in the hope that the sleep will linger. Then he looked up at me and said, 'Daddy, what colour am I?' That woke me up, although the mind was a couple of steps behind everything else.

My initial reaction – anger. Why do I have to live in a country where a three-year-old feels the need to ask that question? Where did he hear about the 'race thing'? Who had he been talking to? I didn't grow up in a place where I had questions like that. I didn't think about it at all. I wasn't oblivious to it, but it wasn't something that I worried about.

The closest I got to a similar question was when I was about sixteen years old. In conversation with my father, I randomly asked how (and why), considering what he had taught me about pan-Africanism and the pride in being Black, he married a white woman – my mother. His response, which had an angry undertone, was that my mother wasn't white, she was my mother. We never had a conversation about my mother's race after that and, in truth, there was never much reason to. I was growing up amidst a potpourri of races; the only thing we really noted was country of origin and heritage, as opposed to skin colour.

Back to my son. I think I mumbled something about his being light brown, but what I was more concerned about was where and how and why he would ask that question. His mother is lighter than the both of us so he didn't ask what colour I was but rather what colour mommy is and, in particular, whether she is white. Having my wits a bit more about me, I said she was pink (I'll probably get into a little trouble saying this, but, oh well). He disagreed until, following what happens after you have done a number two, we walked out of the bathroom and stood on mummy's side of the bed to check her colour – pink cheeks. We had a little chuckle and went back to bed, but it was bothering me, a lot. I fell back asleep with 'we need to leave this country' as my last thought.

Chatting to his nanny at the time, who is also from Lesotho, she admitted that when the older kids in our complex were playing in the play area, they would often talk about so-and-so being white, or Black, or Coloured or Indian. This is suburbia in Johannesburg, so obviously the majority of the children were white, and they were driving this conversation.

When I first started spending time in South Africa, after a year of living in Germany and then settling back in Lesotho, the thing that struck me most was how much skin colour is noted as the first thing when meeting a person – even when it isn't acknowledged. Even the language we use is based on skin colour. White boy. Black girl. Indian guy. It is more than a descriptor and is usually loaded with generalisations and stereotypes. We don't say, the accountant, or the lawyer, or the petrol attendant – well, perhaps the petrol attendant because the assumption is that the only person who would be a petrol attendant is a Black person.

In my first couple of days at the then University of Natal in Durban, someone told me I was Coloured, and I didn't know what that was. Imagine discovering you are 'something' at a time when you are trying to figure out who you are.

The word 'Coloured' is a minefield because, within the countries it has been used, it has totally different references and different spellings.

Through high school, I read a lot about America, the Civil Rights Movement and the plight of the Black man/woman who had been brutally taken there as slaves during the slave trade. I first read Malcolm X's autobiography, as told to Alex Haley, at the age of fifteen and, in my last years of high school, I wrote a mini-thesis for my Theory of Knowledge class on 'Writers in Times of Oppression', with a focus on Black writers from America and South Africa.

According to www.oxforddictionaries.com, 'Colored referring to skin colour is first recorded in the early seventeenth century and was adopted in the US by emancipated slaves as a term of racial pride after the end of the American Civil War. In the US and Britain, it was the accepted term until the 1960s, when it was superseded by Black. The term colored lost favour among Black people during this period and is now widely regarded as offensive except in historical contexts and in particular as part of the name of the NAACP (National Association for the Advancement of Colored People).'

In South Africa, the term Coloured has a different history. It is used to refer to people of mixed-race parentage and heritage rather than, as elsewhere, to refer to African peoples and their descendants (that is, as a synonym for Black). Under apartheid it was imposed as an official racial designation. However, in modern use the term is not generally considered offensive or derogatory.

And so, there I was, as a nineteen-year-old, trying to figure out who I was, as one does at that age, and I had this Coloured thing thrown into the mix and in my face at every turn. The first thing that struck me was the stereotypes associated with Coloured men at the time – drinkers, good-for-nothings and always fighting.

It is tiresome without any real solution to it. The more time I spend living in South Africa, the more it comes into my own vocabulary. Being conscious of this, I try not to do it, with limited success. Having a child made me realise this and having to go through the process of raising him – although he is thirteen at the time of writing this – has forced me to find ways of dealing with it. Add the birth of my daughter, who is light-skinned and has perfectly straight hair, and it became even more confusing.

In the beginning, after that first incident, my reaction, whenever he asked about 'colour', was to react emotionally and tell him that 'it isn't important'. But, for him, and for his friends, I started to realise it was a descriptor without the emotional charge attached to it.

As a result, I had to learn to hold my tongue, take a deep breath and answer calmly whenever he asked questions about 'colour'. I would steer the conversation more towards the character of the human being and how it is important to engage with people on the basis of how they treat you as opposed to making assumptions based on the colour of their skin. Plus, we have the advantage of coming from a family with multiple nationalities and shades, which has made it easier to deal with certain questions.

For example, one day he made a statement about 'brown people's taxis' and how his teacher had said that 'brown people' do not have cars. My older sister is Black, with two Ghanaian parents, and my two younger brothers and sister are also Black, with a Ghanaian father and a Mosotho mother. My older sister is married to a South African from Venda. My younger sister is married to an Englishman and one of my brothers is married to a Mosotho. My response to the 'brown people not having cars' thing was that his grandfather, uncles, aunts and a cousin are all 'brown people' and they all have cars. Problem solved, kinda.

When I took Kweku to the hospital in our neighbourhood for the first time, the nurse entering his details selected Coloured on the dropdown menu when it came to race. I asked her why and proceeded to give her a quick rundown of my heritage and the fact that I am not South African and, therefore, refuse to be boxed in by South Africanisms.

This happens every time I take him to the hospital and every time I end up giving the same spiel. Yet, he is South African, and his mother is Coloured. This I am comfortable with, but, to be honest, the longer it goes on, the harder it is for me to make sense of it in my head.

At the same time, it also involves grappling with how this patriarchal world we have created says that you take your father's nationality or cultural group. Am I being sexist by insisting he be classified, if we need to classify, according to me and my views?

And, if you are wondering, I insist on Other, if it is an option, for my children and myself. If not, then I insist on Black. This is all a tad ironic for me because growing up in a Black family I am the white sheep, and growing up in a Black country I was always Black until I went to university. In navigating the whole race and identity thing at varsity, I had to confront whether, in insisting that I was Black, I was denouncing my white mother and white aunts, uncles and cousins, who have had as important a role in the person I am. If I was simply Black, and Ghanaian, and Mosotho, what about the German in me? I then decided that, if I was to ever define myself racially, I would be bi-racial because I am proud of all the parts of me. 'Other' works just fine, until you come into direct contact with institutions in South Africa that only accommodate the four groups defined during the apartheid era – Black/African, White, Coloured and Asian.

I will say that, at least, the South African census does have Other, which made for a mildly entertaining interaction with a census official in 2011. She had come to our door at around 7 pm while we were having supper, which wasn't the best timing. She was taking too long to fill in the forms, so the missus took over. I was sitting on the couch with Kweku and my mother-in-law watching television. Estelle ticked Coloured for herself and her mother, Black for our housekeeper and then Other for my son and I. The expression on the census lady's face was truly priceless and you could see she had questions but also wanted to get out as quickly as possible, so she stayed silent.

Over the years, my making sense of Coloured has become easier. In getting to know my wife's family and in having Coloured friends, I have come to the conclusion that they are an ethnic group specific to South Africa, with their own rituals, practices and culture. And they are diverse, depending on what part of the country they are from and where the greatest cultural influences come from. At the same time, while I have Coloured people in my family, I do not fall within that group, despite similar physical characteristics – complexion, in particular – in the same way that a dark Black person could be from a multitude of ethnic groups, even from within South Africa.

When I am in Europe, people assume I am bi-racial. When I am in Ghana, I am not confused for anything other than what I am, the product of a Black parent and a white parent. Ghanaians have travelled the world, finding spouses of different races and nationalities for decades.

And for those who feel I have to pick a side, which is something I have often encountered in South Africa, I have come to be comfortable with sitting on the fence. Until the attention is on heritage rather than race, South Africa will always grapple with this. I am alarmed when South African parents of different races call their children Coloured. It feels like a Zulu parent and Sotho parent defining their child as Ndebele. It is about heritage and how we are raised culturally, not about the colour of our skin. Sounds utopian, yes, but how else are those of us sitting in the middle going to make sense of our identities?

Duality

I WROTE this poem many moons ago. When I performed, I wasn't one for explaining my poems as some did, meandering through memory and experience to unpack how the root of that particular poem was inspired by a moment when they were eleven years old and they were denied a scoop of ice cream. Okay, I don't mean to trivialise the journey of others and, when I was on the scene, words were often borne out of deep tragedy and struggle. I just found that by explaining a poem one takes away the opportunity for the listener or reader to find themselves and their experiences in the words.

Coming offstage once, at a small, slightly dingy spot in Johannesburg called Jungle Connection, after sharing some poems that I had poured all of me into, a friend gushed about a particular line in one poem. I felt cheated. I had written all of these lines, taken the time to memorise them and all she was interested in talking about was one line. Once I got over myself, I realised that all you could wish for is your words having an impact, whether one line or twenty.

In English class, we used to analyse poetry. We would go through a work line by line, being taught an interpretation of what the poet meant and the symbolism. Our mark for the subject depended on how well we remembered and explained all of that. With my poems, sometimes I can tell you what was going on around that time, what I was thinking about and what concerned me. Other times, I can't. At times, your guess is as good as mine when it comes to the meaning of the lines.

People have found a connection to joyful memories in poems about pain, and pain in poems about joy. But I will explain this poem because it articulates something that I have grappled with most of my life. My ancestors existed on opposite sides of a racial divide that continues to wreak havoc on the world. This is self-evident in the poem. One of the things that I have always loved about poetry is that one can cloak so much with words, saying one thing but meaning something else. This poem is not one of those poems. I had even thought of editing it – as one is wont to do with old writing and a new, evolved mind – but that would take away from it. How I felt in this moment of time is not that far removed from the fifteen-plus years since I first wrote it.

i stand at the centre of a war
that has been waged for hundreds of years
a war that has been fought
    with burning crosses and thick rope
    with shackles, chains and whips
    with hidden looks and clutched handbags
    with segregation and cultural destruction
    with guns and warplanes
    with bullets and bombs
    with sharp tongues and the devil's eyes
    with fake smiles and darkened hearts
    with misunderstanding and deception
    with hate and cruelty
    with knives in the back and hangmen
    with religion and courtrooms

i stand at the centre of war
that has been televised
commercially edited
    digitally mastered
    and broadcast in stereo

i stand at the centre of a war
where everything is black or white
    yet i am the grey area between warring parties

i am neither black nor white
    and yet i am both
  i am neither african nor european
    and yet i am both

  i am your future
    devoid of a side to pick
  i am your hope
    devoid of your understanding
  i am your greatest fear
    and i am your wildest aspiration
  i am the merger of your strengths
    and i am the failure of your weaknesses
  i am a symbol of your love
    and a victim of your hatred
  i am the unification of your desire to separate
    and separate from your desire to unify
  i am a power unto myself
    and the product of your power
  i am so much
    and yet represent so little

i exist in the midst of the confusion
    your birthed me into
    because i am the product
    of two factions stuck
    on extreme poles of reality

On the edge

I READ Thomas Hardy's *Far from the Madding Crowd* when I was in high school and the title has always stuck with me, although it is probably as much for the idea of a 'madding crowd' as it was for embarrassing myself in English class because of it. We were supposed to have written a composition on it and, because I hadn't actually read it, I read the first two chapters and the last chapter and wrote an essay that totally missed the mark.

To feel alone amidst the madding crowd can be a painful place to be. And, for large portions of my life, that is how I have felt. Alone, sometimes lonely, amongst people, even with people who are supposed to be my people. This goes as far back as I can remember, to the photograph of me, in the middle of people, as a toddler.

The concept of belonging is strange. The world can see you as belonging, but more important is how you see yourself. I have never felt like I fully belonged, anywhere. In my family, I am the white sheep, the only one with a white mother, the only one with European heritage, my mother's only child. We weren't raised that way. We were all Baffoe children, raised as siblings without any 'step' in the mix. But I still felt different because I was different. And there were elements of their lives, beyond the home, that I wasn't part of.

I was fortunate to travel at a young age and attend such a culturally diverse school that my influences have always been broad, overlapping but not always in line with the people I grew up with.

At varsity, I was the Sesotho-speaking, not-Coloured guy who lived in res, surrounded by and socialising with mainly Black people. I could never run away from me because there is only one half-German, half-Ghanaian Mosotho with a typical Ghanaian name. Plus, culturally, I am a mishmash of all of these, often drawing from what makes sense to me and discarding what doesn't.

If someone said they had heard of me, it was probably me they were talking about and not a case of mistaken identity.

I was considered 'a pretty boy' for most of my adolescence and even into my twenties, and that also drew attention when I preferred to lurk on the edges, entering spaces quietly and sussing out the space before I actually engaged.

Getting involved in the poetry scene forced me to learn how to stand up in front of people, and being involved in the media, especially *Destiny Man*, meant that I had to get comfortable with hosting and speaking at a range of events. I still get very nervous before I have to get up in front of people and like to arrive early just to get comfortable with the energy in the room.

Poetry and *Destiny Man* brought with them a bit of public profile in South Africa, and yet, despite being considered South African in some spaces, when it boils down to it, I am a 'foreigner', which often crops up when it comes to doing any type of work that would be easier if I was BEE-compliant. I have heard the comment 'by the way, you are not South Africa' countless times and it always reminds me of my otherness.

I have worked in so many different industries that I could never define myself according to my job and never quite belonged to any specific community, which has allowed me to traverse multiple spaces. Estelle used to throw me surprise birthday parties, to my chagrin, and the thing that always stood out was that the people invited often came from very different worlds and would, under normal circumstances, not cross paths. This was, of course, before social media.

Being an immigrant in Lesotho, I have been considered not Mosotho enough. Having grown up outside of Ghana my whole life, in some quarters, I am not Ghanaian enough. There have been instances, particularly when

I have accomplished things deemed of value, when I have been claimed by those places. The Germans have never claimed me, however, but there's still time.

There was a time when all of this really bothered me, but, as I have grown older, I have learned to embrace my otherness because that is what has enabled me to do some of the things I have done and given me perspectives that help me contribute to those around me in ways that others can't.

This idea of being other, of not quite belonging anywhere yet belonging everywhere is now a source of pride.

Small-town boy

DESPITE HAVING travelled extensively as a child and in adulthood, I am a small-town boy at heart. I like the comfort of familiarity that growing up in a small town, and eventually small city, brings. I think it has a lot to do with being recognised for you, within a particular context.

Maseru in the 1980s and 1990s was a fascinating place, especially with the diversity that apartheid brought. Companies and embassies and the like established a presence in Lesotho because of the proximity to South Africa, without being seen to be interacting with the country during sanctions. I went to school with the children of diplomats, business people and expatriates.

Until the first democratic elections in South Africa in 1994, it felt as if every country had an embassy or high commission in Maseru, and the United Nations and European Union had a big presence. After 1994, a lot of the embassies moved across, with a handful maintaining offices in Lesotho. We went from being able to apply for visas to most places in the world in Maseru to having to make the trek to Johannesburg or Pretoria (Tshwane).

As a result of the fishbowl nature of Maseru and being surrounded by what felt like a hostile country, the friendships that were forged during my primary- and high-school years and beyond have endured in one form or another since. For many friends who spent time there during the 1980s, Lesotho continues to hold a special place for them. And the beauty of the advent of social media is that we have been able to reconnect years later and there have been some friends who have been able to visit.

In some ways, we have grown up together, at a distance. Sadly, this has been most evident with the story of a friend, Michelle, from Canada who battled with and succumbed to cancer in 2020. We went through the decade-long journey with her as she sought treatment around the world, experiencing her highs and lows as ours, primarily through Facebook. When she decided that she wasn't going to keep up the fight, a German friend reached out and many of us sent farewell video messages.

I have carried this small-town way of living to Joburg where I have lived in the same area for close to twenty years, eventually becoming friendly with the people at the neighbourhood petrol station and the supermarket as well as my neighbours in the complexes we have lived in. I like being able to go to places and having the waiter confirm my order as opposed to asking for it.

I will say, though, as I have gone deeper into suburbia, I still find it strange how we can live alongside each other without getting to know each other. The sense of community sometimes feels forced when it should be a given.

When Kweku was born, it was especially challenging because my family was in Lesotho and Estelle's mother was on the other side of the city. It was a pleasure when she moved in and stayed with us until she passed away.

In Maseru, when I needed something, there was always someone who could provide it, outside of the more formal channels. In Joburg, I had to build those networks, yet it can still be difficult because we are so spread out. There was a point where we had to change our lifestyle and our routines, especially after the kids were born, because that support wasn't there.

We have a circle of friends as a family who have become family, and, once again, I live the small-town boy life. There are parts of the city I never get to because they are too far out. I guess the advantage of a city like Joburg is that, within each area, there is access to all that one needs.

Unpatriotic

I HAVE lived in South Africa for about twenty years, first on a residence permit and then as a permanent resident. I applied for a work permit when I initially moved to Joburg, having started my IT company with a South Africa partner and two South African employees, but I was turned down twice. Whichever immigration official was processing my application decided that the business would not succeed, or at least that was the reasoning given.

Getting married to a South African eventually smoothed the process – and no, that's not why I married her. When I went to apply for my permanent resident permit, Estelle had to come with me for an interview to confirm that it was not a marriage of convenience. At that stage, we had been married and living together for over two years, so the interview never happened.

Recently, I realised that I have lived in South Africa for nearly as long as I lived in Lesotho and yet I feel no overwhelming sense of patriotism to the country. I would like to think that it has had no bearing on whatever small contributions I have made to and in the country. I will always be vested in South Africa, one, because it is my home – at least for now – and, two, it is the birthplace and home country of three of the most important people in my life, Estelle and my children.

I do often wonder where the lack of patriotism comes from. I know of many others who assimilated and are not forthright about where they originally come from. Sometimes I wish I could simply switch it on as they seemingly have, but I cannot. I love elements of the county. I consider myself a Joburger through and through and, for all its challenges, I love the city – it will forever be one of my favourite cities.

Is it the challenges that I have faced, getting my permits, getting support or the lack thereof? Is it the xenophobia, or more specifically, Afrophobia, that often feels like a fixed undercurrent to all parts of society, sometimes covert, increasingly overt? Is it being told repeatedly, especially in my early years in the country, that South Africa is better than all other African countries because of the infrastructure and development, which I consider a legacy of apartheid? Is it the jokes about how Lesotho does not warrant being a country and should just be another province of South Africa, negating its history and the history of its people?

Perhaps it is all of the above. Perhaps it is also because I spent my formative years in Maseru, arriving as a child and leaving as a man. Ghana and Germany were always easy, even though I never lived in either, except for the year in Germany after high school. I was born in Germany, my mother was German, my father lived there for many years and I visited relatives often as a child. I would be put on a plane alone and shipped off to visit for several Christmases. I had a German passport until my early twenties. It is a part of my heritage. My father was born in Ghana. My name is Ghanaian. I interacted with a lot of Ghanaians growing up and I was raised with that culture and lens. Being a football fan, I have supported the national teams, the Black Stars and Die Mannschaft, for as long as I can remember.

I was raised in and by Lesotho. My father naturalised when I was a teenager and that is still home, even with him no longer there, although that is where he is buried. My experiences, perspectives and culture come from there. Perhaps it is because I spent the years that laid the foundation for the man I am in Lesotho and came to South Africa as an adult, fending for himself.

A cousin once said, when I was complaining about South Africa, that the country had given me so much, including a wife. My retort was that I had to work hard for everything I gained, including the wife, sometimes twice as hard as everyone around me.

When I performed poetry, there were gigs that I wasn't booked for because I wasn't South African, and the promoters were concerned about the optics. In business, there were projects I was contributing to where it became a problem when looking at shareholding because I was a 'foreigner'. I'm not complaining, I am a big believer in the importance of things like Black Economic Empowerment to level the very unequal playing field. Sometimes it has felt like I am being taken advantage of, where the value I create isn't reciprocated.

I would like to think that I have contributed in my little way to the country that has been my home for twenty years, a country that I would like to see flourish. I have, in some quarters, been acknowledged and recognised for those contributions. It is weird to feel a part of something and divorced from it simultaneously.

Someday, I will find the answer to this. In the meantime, I continue to try to contribute, to participate, to live.

I'm an African

YEARS AGO, in a Twitter discussion about being African, I was told by a Black South African man that I could call myself African because 'Nelson Mandela said that Coloureds could be African'. Fortunately, this conversation wasn't face to face because I suspect that my response wouldn't have been as tame as it was online. My response was that I did not need affirmation from Nelson Mandela to validate the nature or extent of my African-ness.

That statement, coming from someone in a country that has 'Africa' in its name, yet its people still talk of 'going to Africa' like it is another planet, made my stomach turn. At times, it feels like South Africa feels conveniently African. Part of the collective one moment, violent towards 'Africans' who are taking jobs, women and housing or are drug dealers, human traffickers and criminals, the next.

A friend, who is South African, calls the country 'Africa Lite' or 'Diet Africa'. When you visit the main cities, you get a sort of sanitised version of Africa. Even 'going to the bush'/on safari is a nicely packaged African experience without the sights, sounds and true challenges of how people really live.

South Africa still has a way to go in figuring out what a South African identity is, made even more complex by the history and diversity of ethnic groups, cultures, religions and races within the country. Sometimes, when I am particularly frustrated by things, I have to remind myself of that. There is a tragic legacy that the country is still working its way out of, and there will, of course, be growing pains and missteps coupled with small triumphs.

But to be told by a South African that I have permission to call myself African is where I draw the line. Kwame Nkrumah, the African leader who greatly influenced my father, and me, by extension, said, 'I am not African because I was born in Africa but because Africa was born in me.'

While I wasn't born in Africa, I have lived on the continent since I was a baby. I was born into a household where pan-African ideals underpinned the way we lived and I continue to try to live in a way that is about putting a spotlight on Africans and African history.

My being African was never in doubt, until I came to South Africa, where the idea of race supersedes everything else and African is now used to describe a race. When you look at any data on South Africa's demographics, race groups are divided into Black African, Coloured, Indian/Asian and white.

I first came face to face with this at university. Up to that point, I never had to fill in race on forms. In my first year of university, forced to select a race on my registration forms, I selected Black. When I received my forms to update for registration for second year, I discovered that it had been switched to Coloured. I corrected it and ticked Black again, only for it to have been switched back to Coloured when I was registering for third year. It was the same administrator every year who had been making the change after I had submitted my forms, so, in that third and final year, I took a photograph of my family from the recent Christmas holidays.

I went through every person in the picture and asked her how she would classify them. She agreed that they were all Black. My question was then who was she to decide that I couldn't define myself as Black, especially considering they did not have Bi-racial or Other on the forms?

It can be tiresome trying to make sense of and navigate identity in South Africa. In a society that still needs to find itself, one gets pulled in multiple directions. I consider myself African with every fibre of my being. That is how my father raised me, that is where my attention is and that is where my allegiance lies, even with the different African countries that made me, including South Africa.

Home that isn't home

MY IDEA of home has evolved over the years. Moving to Joburg, it wasn't until I got married that I considered the city and the apartment we initially lived in as home. Yet, when I drove to Maseru, I was going home and, until my father passed away, I would refer to it as such, even when I hadn't been there for a year or two. Actually, I still talk of Maseru has 'hae' or 'makaya' – home.

It was always a little weird driving from Joburg to Maseru and returning to Joburg; I was leaving home to go home and returning from home to home. As the road dipped down towards the Maseru Bridge border gate, a sense of calm would come over me. And, seeing the last petrol station on the outskirts of Joburg, as I drove into the city, gave me the same feeling.

But I found a rhythm in it.

And then I went to Ghana with my father and brother Kweku at the age of 38, in December 2008. I had last been there as a young child and have no memories of that trip.

After the 2008 visit, I found it extremely difficult to articulate how I felt about Ghana. It felt like home. Accra had changed immensely since my father grew up there; it was a little surreal both experiencing, for the first time, where he grew up after being separated from it for my whole life, and watching him rediscover the changed city, trying to remember where everything was. It was fascinating seeing him go back through memories of a time half a century before and experiencing that journey with him.

We went back together again twice the following year, and I tweeted:

7 Apr 2009: In the land of my father, I inhale the spirit of my ancestors and let it cleanse me from within.

8 Apr 2009: Returned to a home I've never been to, and yet I feel at home. There are moments when there are no words.

2 Jun 2009: It speaks to my soul, this strange land that feels like home, this is where my ancestors lie and where they guide me from.

Is it possible to feel at home in a place you have never lived, ever? There is that feeling in your chest and there is what people say. I am proud of the fact that my father kept with tradition and ensured that we all have Ghanaian names, which we all use. It probably helped smooth the journey through Ghana because, when people heard my name, the general reaction was welcome home.

Plus, I am not an anomaly in Ghana. Ghanaians have travelled the world since before independence, finding partners of different nationalities and races, and producing offspring.

But, at the same time, there is the discussion in the shadows of being or not being Ghanaian enough. It is such a difficult one because there are no clear criteria. My father was Ghanaian, by birth, and then changed nationalities in his forties. I was automatically Ghanaian by nationality when I was born but never carried a Ghanaian passport – I was on my father's – and eventually had a German passport. When my father naturalised in Lesotho, I was about sixteen years old and I too became a citizen.

There is your nationality according to the laws of different countries and there is what you feel in your heart. And my allegiance has always been to Lesotho, Ghana and Germany as my homeland, fatherland and motherland. There is where my ancestors come from, and how I linked to them spiritually and physically through lineage, and there is the country that raised me. And, whether I like it or not, there is the country where I have carved out a space for myself and made a name for myself, South Africa. Each one is a part of who I am and each one serves as a home of sorts.

The watchers

There are those who watch over us
They go by many names
They guide us
Whether we are on the right path
Or go wonderfully astray
Their presence is in the moments
Awake or asleep
There are those who watch over us
Ancestors are their names

The painful bite of heroes

IT WAS a straightforward composition to write. Choose a hero and write about why they were/are your hero. It was an easy choice for me. My father. He stood above all the others. Bob Marley. Malcolm X. Bruce Lee. Muhammad Ali. They were my heroes because of him. I had learned of and from them at his feet.

I was in my early teens. My father rarely engaged in the mechanics of my schooling. He was too busy raising five children, navigating the transition from academia to entrepreneurship, dealing with life. The only time we talked about my performance at school was when the dreaded report arrived at the end of the year.

I wasn't a bad student but I wasn't an exceptional one either. My teachers seemed to have come together to agree that, if I focused more, I could do so much better. That never even clutched at the shirt tails of my father's high standards. If I received a mark of 95 per cent (which rarely happened), his view was, considering I was so close, I should have just got 100 per cent. It was only 5 per cent more.

I brought the composition home, proud. I can't remember how I did, marks wise, but I hungered for a pat on the shoulder from my father. He was my hero and his validation meant more than anything else.

His response was restrained, at first, until he saw that I had listed his place of birth. Not Accra but Nkoranza. To say he was displeased is an understatement. I still don't know why, but, out of the entire writing, he was angry that I had listed the place where he was born as different from what he said. I had found the place in one of his old passports.

I have always taken pride in my heritage, where I was born, the journey my people have taken to bring me to today. With hindsight, I realise that my father spent a lifetime looking forward, not backwards. In a way, he was trying to get out of and as far away from his early years as possible and, once he did, he was never interested in reconnecting with it.

What I knew and what I now know aren't that different – still limited. He was his mother and father's only child, together. Both my grandparents had families and my grandmother definitely had other children. Who they are and who their children are, I haven't got a clue.

I remember a Ghanaian woman in Lesotho insisting that she was my aunt. I grew up calling everyone Uncle and Aunty, so I replied in the affirmative. It was at an uncle's funeral, and she said with great conviction and passion, 'I am your father's cousin', looking directly at my father. I don't think he even shrugged.

With the advent of social media, Facebook in particular, I decided to start finding Baffoes. It became a terse conversation with my father whenever I mentioned that I had found a Baffoe who we were possibly related to. My father's standard response was, 'I have spent my whole life trying to build a life for my children. All extended family will do is try to exploit you, taking advantage of the things that you have accomplished.'

He had sung this song right through my teens. I would remind him that I was a grown man and not that easy to take advantage of, plus it wasn't like I had much anyway. Even when we started visiting Ghana more often, the people we interacted with were not family in the traditional sense of the word but, rather, friendships he had built over the years.

Now that he is gone, most of my relationships in Ghana are the same friends who have become family, except for one cousin who I have got to know over the years.

While I have been able to build a family beyond my siblings and friends, I do still lament that I was never able to get my father to reconnect with whatever family we have in Ghana, even if it was just about knowing who they are. The elders serve as the link in the chain as the documenters of family history, and most of them are gone. Sadly, one can't always trust those who reach out because you never know what their intentions are.

My father still remains my hero, my mentor, my guide. That will never change. Even when some memories bite, painfully.

A list of names

Every night
I recite a litany of names
For those gone
But forever present
The list seems longer

Where have the grandfathers all gone?

MY CHILDREN have a gang of grandmothers, Estelle's aunts, my aunts and collected mother figures. But no grandfathers. Estelle's father passed away when Kweku was still a baby. Kweku had my father for nine years and Ayanna had him for five years. It is also a little strange that their actual paternal grandmother is someone in the pictures. When she was younger, we would constantly have to remind Ayanna who Grandma Elfi was. The fact that she was my mother was often difficult to grasp, for both of them, because it wasn't someone they ever interacted with.

I grew up without my grandparents on both sides. Both my grandfathers died before I was born and my grandmothers not too long after I was born. It isn't a relationship that has ever made any sense to me. The closest I had to grandparents were my Opa and Oma in Germany who, I was to discover when I was much older, were the parents of one of my mother's close friends who took her in when she was living in Hamburg.

I guess I did have a grandfather for a period. This was a time when we used to go to Germany regularly and always visited them. He took me to see the Bee Gees' version of the movie *Sgt. Pepper's Lonely Hearts Club Band*. He would take me to the park. He would carry me on his shoulders in the snow when it got too cold, and I too tired. I remember losing a tooth eating an apple in their home, with Opa and Oma comforting me because I had swallowed the tooth.

When Opa died, I hadn't seen him for a couple of years. I was in my teens and my father told me of his death in passing. I was obviously sad, but I still remember feeling confused. I don't know whether it was the setting – my father had friends over – or because it was night-time. There was a darkness, although I didn't cry. All I have is a frozen memory of the moment. Nothing before and nothing after.

I watched friends with their grandparents. I have watched my children watch their friends with their grandfathers. Although I can't change it, I wish I could. There is something about the love of grandad that is beautiful to watch. My father used to drive from Maseru to Sasolburg in the Free State just to attend my nephews's and niece's grandparents day at kindergarten. He made one of Ayanna's and a couple of Kweku's.

Sadly, they won't have a grandfather to be that shoulder for them any more. Grandmothers, yes. But the love of a grandfather, no.

Talk the talk

LANGUAGE AND culture are connected. To speak a person's language is to gain insight into a person's culture, their perspectives, the context within which they interact with the world. I learned how to speak Sesotho on the streets of Maseru and at home. My brief stint in Sesotho class in primary school ended, literally, in tears. I struggled to fit in. I understood too much to be in the beginner's class but not enough to be in the more advanced class for born Sesotho speakers.

I decided to switch to French and our Sesotho teacher, who was much feared, told me never to come back to her class since I had decided to give it up. Hence the tears. I must have been nine years old.

But, growing up in Maseru, in a Sesotho-speaking country, in a home where it was spoken nearly as much as English, I learned how to speak the language relatively fluently, even though my reading and writing continue to be dismal.

It has been a useful skill to have, especially in the time that I have spent in South Africa, although, because I don't speak it as often in the time I have been here, there are moments when words feel strange around my tongue and my vocabulary has dipped. Because language in Johannesburg is often diluted, my Sesotho words and pronunciations always set me apart.

There is a novelty to someone who is not expected to speak a language speaking that particular language. In South Africa, my skin tone and hair texture mean that more people expect me to speak Afrikaans, which I don't speak, than what is often termed 'vernacular', or 'vernac', for short. I have become used to the funny facial expressions when I do speak Sesotho but draw the line at the vernac thing. I find it weird that people would bundle a bunch of languages under this umbrella and will often retort with 'I don't speak vernac' – it isn't an actual language – but Sesotho. A friend once remarked that, when I speak Sesotho, it feels like one has been transported into a dubbed kung-fu flick and, before he got used to my speaking it, he kept expecting to see someone behind me speaking, while I just moved my lips.

Speaking Sesotho has made life much smoother. The number of times the ability to speak a language other than English in South Africa has helped are countless. From calming down a cabin crew transport driver at the airport after he reversed into my car to applying for a passport for Kweku at Home Affairs; it makes for a more pleasant experience, generally.

When I was in high school, for some random reason, there was talk of Afrikaans being offered. My father was one of those very much against it. At Kweku's school, from Grade 4, they had to choose their second language, having studied isiZulu and Afrikaans as additional languages up to that point. There was no Sesotho available, so he has been doing isiZulu ever since. And Ayanna as well. Afrikaans was not an option, even though Estelle speaks that.

It has been a challenge because Estelle and I don't speak isiZulu. I do have basic understanding but not enough to help with schoolwork. I constantly try to impress upon Kweku the importance of being able to speak an 'indigenous' (for lack of a better word) language, plus isiZulu is the most spoken language in South Africa.

I find that, when learning a language, it is best to have some theoretical knowledge and the ability to construct sentences, coupled with constant exposure to the spoken part. Yet, while my children are getting a strong theoretical foundation in the classroom, speaking it is the harder part, even living in a country where the language is spoken. Our circle of friends comes from a variety of backgrounds and speak different languages, so we tend to speak English as the common denominator.

If that has to do, that has to do. I still struggle to understand why, with the country's and the language's history, schools still insist on Afrikaans as a second language. Children died for the right to speak their own languages and not be forced to speak Afrikaans, yet here we are.

CREATIVITY

Fail, rinse, repeat

I FAILED my final year in high school. I have never admitted that to anyone, myself included. I went through the British school system, doing the International General Certificate of Secondary Education (IGCSE) curriculum, and, after doing Form Five in 1988, I did two years of Form Six in its new structure – the International Baccalaureate (IB) diploma.

Traditionally, for A-Levels (Form Six), you studied two to three subjects over the two years. This was equivalent to first year of university so students often did the subjects that would then be their majors in university. With IB, you studied six subjects, three at higher level and three at subsidiary level.

I failed English, which I was doing as my mother tongue at higher level, and mathematics, which I was doing at subsidiary level. Maths was understandable. The only time my father ever wished me luck was when I was going to write that exam. This from a man who believed more in hard work and the power of the mind than luck.

Two things happened that have enabled me to essentially lie to myself for 30 years. Firstly, I was in Germany at the time my results came out, so I didn't have to repeat the school year with the class that came after me. And, secondly, because IB was, and still is, an international diploma, I found an IB school in Hamburg, just over 120 kilometres from where I was in Oldenburg. As a result, I could rewrite the exams far away from anyone who knew me, without the stigma of 'failure' attached to it.

I remember driving with my host father to register and get all the necessary coursework to study. A few weeks later, I took the train to go write my exams. I wish I could say I approached this second round with a sense of urgency, but, staying alone in a youth hostel, I spent that first afternoon wandering around the red-light district of Reeperbahn – a real eye-opener for a small-town boy – the day before my exams. I did, however, pass the two subjects.

Failure is a funny thing. Because of those struggles in high school, and because I was always a mid-table (football reference) student, I weirdly came to university without a fear of failure. My attitude was also greatly influenced by having worked full-time for the period between returning from Germany in July 1991 to going to university in February 1992. When you put effort into a proposal for a project and it does not materialise, you start to learn that sometimes you won't succeed at something, regardless of how much effort you put in and how much you think you deserve it.

My approach was 'lose the battle, win the war', although I can only say that with hindsight. At the time, I was less confident about what I was doing with life. I did know, however, that I couldn't not complete my degree and graduate – it wasn't in my father's lexicon – but, considering I was already working during holidays in the family business, I also knew that I would have a job when I finished school.

Having worked also gave me a lot of practical knowledge to draw from when it came to the coursework. I knew why I was at varsity, primarily to get the theoretical knowledge to build on what my father taught me, and I approached it, partially, like a project for a client, although I was probably a bit more lackadaisical than I would be doing paid-for work. All I needed to do was pass each year and, after three years, walk away with a degree.

A close friend of mine, who I met in the first week of varsity, came from high school as one of the top students, in mathematics particularly, not just for school but for his province. When we were given our first maths test back, which we had both failed (not surprising on my side considering my history with the subject and the reality that I was doing it for the credits and because I had to), he spent the next hour poring over the test to see where he went wrong. He would do this for every test. I eventually got bored and would go play pool with the guys in our residence. Once it was done, I didn't want anything more to do with a test.

It became a self-fulfilling prophecy for him. The more pressure he put on himself, the harder each test became, which he would struggle with, and then pore over the results again, on and on. Eventually, my friend decided to take a step back and redo one or two first-year subjects in second year and came back stronger.

I, on the other hand, did what I needed to do – no, not cheat – to get through. Before the start of second year, I had to rewrite maths and accounting because I received just under 50 per cent. Someone discovered that, for maths, they put the same type of question on the same page in each exam – they did change this after this particular set of exams. A struggle I had through high school and into university was always determining which formula to use for which type of question. Armed with this new knowledge, all I did was memorise the formula for each page. With accounting, I memorised the structure of an income statement and balance sheet and, when I sat down to start the exam, wrote each out on a blank sheet of paper before I even looked at the questions.

My theory was you didn't have to get the right answer or have your balance sheet actually balance; as long as my workings were above 50 per cent, I was good. They were and I was, passing accounting comfortably the second time around. Not wanting to test the boundaries of my 'good fortune', I dropped both maths and accounting in my second year, having received the necessary credits for both.

My father would often bemoan my willingness to take what he termed 'the lazy man's way'. In my mind, it was a smart way of working; it was about finding the shortest route possible to the desired outcome. It was a point of contention even when I finished university and was working full-time with him.

It didn't help that my father was a workaholic. I never felt that I worked hard enough, even when I was putting in fourteen- to fifteen-hour days because he always seemed to be working. When I was in high school, the light from his bedroom would reflect on the wall above my bed, through a little window above the door, from 2 am. He would take a short nap at about 6 am, wake up at 6.30 am and get ready to take us to school. He kept this up until he had a heart attack at 55, when I was back home and working full-time. He slowed down a bit after this, but not much.

When I also started putting in the long hours, the number of times I was accused of taking the easy way out declined. When we ran our newspaper, *Southern Star*, I would get to bed at midnight on a Thursday, wake up at 3.30 am, cross the border at 4 am to be at the printers in Kroonstad, 220 kilometres away, by 6 am.

It took me leaving home, moving to Johannesburg and growing older for me to understand that working oneself to the bone is both not sustainable and not the best way of operating. The transition from living-to-work to working-to-live has been a long and sometime arduous journey that I am still on.

I have had what some would consider multiple failures since I ventured to the City of Gold in search of my version of a pot of gold at the end of a rainbow. I was once interviewed on a show called *Take* 5 about 'bouncing back from failure' after leaving BAKA Consulting in 1999/2000. The presenter could not understand why I did not consider it a failure and, therefore, did not see me as the best person to talk to about the subject.

In my head, it was simple. I had gone into a business. My business partner and I did not see eye to eye in terms of both the operations of the business and the direction we were taking so I volunteered to walk away. Initially, he was to buy me out of my half of the business and supply me with a super-charged PC. Things were tough so I gave up my share at no cost and later, when things were even tougher, I gave him back the computer. Yet, I have never looked at it as a 'failure' but rather a project that did not work. I simply moved on.

That was not the first time and I doubt it is the last time. I have become quite comfortable with walking away from things that are not working without qualms or a second thought. Kwame Nkrumah once said, 'Forwards ever, backwards never', and my high-school motto was 'pele ea pele' (loosely translated as 'always forwards' or 'keep it up'). I have taken this to heart and would rather devote energy to moving forwards, while learning from what some would consider failure, than lamenting or wallowing.

I would like to think that failing English and mathematics all those years ago helped me develop this mindset and approach, which have ensured a modicum of peace of mind as I work and live and evolve.

The end of days

LIVING THROUGH a global pandemic that has and continues to alter how we live as human beings, I often wonder what my father would have thought of it all. In some ways, I am grateful that he didn't have to deal with it, considering that he would have been in his mid-eighties, not in the best health and living in a country without sufficient health facilities.

I do, however, miss what would have been insightful, interesting discussions about human behaviour, nature, politics, institutions and everything in-between. I often think back on something he said to me in 1999, in the lead-up to the 'millennium bug' that was to hit when our calendars were to shift over to 1 January 2000.

At its most basic, the Y2K bug was a programming flaw where computers would interpret the 00 in 2000 as 1900 and wreak havoc on systems globally. It does seem laughable now that I look back, considering how entrenched technology is in our world today compared to then. But, in those days, I would get easily caught up in things, in moments, in experiences, in predictions.

I had just finished my final exams for my commerce degree in December 1994. I had a job lined up at Unilever in the detergent department as an assistant brand manager. I had been groomed to work in the family business, but I wanted the space to build my own life outside of my father's shadow, so I signed the contract. I applied for a work permit before returning home for the holidays. The expectation was that it would take a month or two to get my work permit, following which I would relocate to Durban.

In the meantime, my father decided to start an IT company because he had established a business relationship with Denel Informatics. Denel has a varied history as a part of the South African apartheid government's military cabal, but, after the elections in 1994, it was split into Infoplan, which sold military equipment, and Denel Informatics.

Denel Informatics was looking to establish a presence outside South Africa and, as a result, we became their official business partner for Lesotho. This meant that I had access to fleet, hospital and library management software and the spectrum of identification technologies and biometrics. I spent a couple of days at Denel's head office in Pretoria being schooled in the different offerings. I also spent a day learning how to repair computers – basically, taking out each component and replacing it with a new one until something worked.

Still very Afrikaner and still very white, it was amusing watching the subtle reactions of all the business unit heads when they discovered that the person they were presenting to was a young, 'non-white' (in their eyes) man with a bald head, earrings and a gold X medallion hanging round his neck, and clad in all black.

Two months became three then four and I ended up not going back to Durban. The South African government was taking so long to give me a work permit, and after I applied three times – twice in Durban and once in Lesotho – it stopped making sense to uproot myself. I was intricately involved in the family businesses once more and, as my father said, I was young, had done two years of Business Information Systems and was able to figure out this 'computer stuff'.

In those early years, I had a PC in my bedroom with a phone line connected to the modem, which dialled into an internet service provider in Bloemfontein because we had none in Lesotho. To connect to the early versions of the internet, using Alta Vista browser, meant it was an international call. Gradually, I submerged myself in this world of technology and discovered the millennium bug, which threw me into a panic. I wrote papers on it and presented to departments in government. My biggest concern was that the West would make sure that they were fine, but who was going to worry about a small country like Lesotho? I mean, most people didn't even know where it was.

There was no sense of urgency. I kept bumping my head against walls that were, to me, fuelled by ignorance and wilfulness. I was getting frustrated, voicing my disgust and irritation to my father constantly until, one day, he sat me down and asked me, 'What will happen if the Y2K bug hits?' I replied that computer systems would break down, planes would fall out of the sky, even our PCs would stop working.

His response was that we had lived before all of these things and we would continue to, making do and finding new ways of living if it did happen. He had faith in human resilience and our ability to evolve, regardless of the circumstances. I didn't get it then, but it is something that carries me now. Sadly, it often brings with it unnecessary tragedy and suffering; nonetheless it has ensured that I approach life with hope.

I dream of writing happy poems

POETRY: THE one element of English class that was usually met with groans. Sitting in a classroom in a small African town in a small African country, learning the poetry of old Englishmen was perhaps not the best way to be introduced to it. Or maybe it was because there was a right and a wrong answer to every interpretation of each sentence. Our teachers never let us find the meaning in the poems, meaning that was relevant to us.

Yet, as I navigated my way through each form, I eventually discovered in Form Six that I enjoyed writing poetry. It feels like I have always written my thoughts down regularly; as mentioned, my father always said that if you wanted to make sense of something, you should write it down. Gradually, the sentences became shorter, occasionally rhymed, and became poems. I started filling notebooks, files and folders with these poems. I would write little poems for my high-school girlfriend.

What also helped was that the English curriculum was diverse, including everything from Indian novels, African short stories and Chinese poetry (translated, of course) to the writing of Thomas Hardy, Athol Fugard, William Shakespeare and Geoffrey Chaucer (in original language). We studied the work of Sophocles (*Antigone*) and the French poet Jacques Prévert. I must confess that for years I did not use capitals anywhere in my poetry because of Jacques Prévert.

Our French teacher said the reason why he didn't use capital letters in his poetry, and his regular reference to birds, was because, for him, they represented freedom. I don't know how accurate this is, but it is probably the only thing that has stuck with me all these years later. My reason, other than his influence, was much simpler: I liked the way the words look, uncapitalised.

From that point though, poetry became my therapy. Being a teenage boy who did angst very well, I had more than enough to write about. Having moods that swung like a coked-up pendulum, there were always enough down moments to inspire dark, morose poetry of the woe-is-me type.

Fast-forward a decade or so, I am now living in Johannesburg. I have jumped into the burgeoning poetry scene, spending many a night on open-mic stages baring my soul. Things are tough. I am making ends meet, barely. My father wants me to move back to Lesotho but that would mean that I failed when I finally left home at the age of 27, so I double down and keep writing.

I party hard, indulge in substances beyond alcohol. I come home on most weekends to my one-bed, two-chair and one-pot townhouse and write poetry to the sounds of Santana's 'Black Magic Woman', the page lit by a single candle. When I wake up in the morning, I find that I have written lines on top of lines, making the poems illegible.

I eventually move in with my aunt because I can't afford to maintain my own place. I walk out of the business, with nothing to show for the year or so that I was involved with it because of differences with my business partner, eventually giving him everything.

The poetry is flowing. I am writing three to four poems a day. There is enough darkness to feed the muse and she is generous with her offerings in return. Some of the poems are actually decent. I end up in rehab. As part of the process of getting off white powder and white tablets, I do a number of courses that are designed to help me find myself and I find a version of me that is less destructive. I am clean, to a degree. I quit drugs and alcohol but hang onto my cigarettes. The muse moves on to the next troubled soul.

Some of my favourite writers were troubled, for various reasons, and homosexual – Oscar Wilde, Truman Capote and James Baldwin. I would often wonder whether I would be able to write again because, while I was never gay, I was always troubled. Now that I had put my troubles behind me and was, for the first time, optimistic about the future, I wondered whether the words would come.

I read a tweet once by Airea D. Matthews. I don't know her, but the tweet reminded me of this time. She said, 'The hardest poem to write is one of joy. I don't know why. Maybe because we sense it in our bodies as loss? Maybe because as soon as joy comes something has to replace it? Maybe because we privilege the thieves of joy above joy itself? Maybe stop doing that.'

How true this is. Learning how to write poems while happy was harder than learning how to write. This doesn't imply that every poem will be happy, that it will be about joy. Sometimes, it's about being able to tap into the emotions and thoughts from a happy place. At other times, those thoughts are not happy and the words that reflect them are sombre, sad and painful, because, sometimes, poems need to be about the darkness. But you need to be able to access them without being pulled back into the abyss.

There was a time when the discussion amongst the poets in my circle was centred on our being the 'voices for the voiceless'. I disagreed, not because I didn't feel pain or empathy but rather because, while I could empathise, I could never be their voice because my context was different to theirs. I have grown up and lived with an element of privilege that I felt and feel, which makes it hard for me to speak for those who haven't had that. I can express how it makes me feel, I can be a voice drawing attention to their plight, and hopefully do what I can to alleviate it, but I can never speak for them. I can highlight their troubles, although it will always be from a position of privilege.

I found that poetic voice, eventually: writing poems that spoke to the pain and the joy, remembering, atoning, celebrating, sharing. And then I lost it again. I lost it because … life, responsibility. But the poems are there. Just beneath the surface. Happy poems. Sad poems. Poems about love and life. Poems that speak my reality. And one day, they will resurface.

This I know. And yet, sometimes, I dream of writing happy poems.

The I in writing

THE PROCESS of writing a book about one's life experiences and views on the world is one that has forced me to confront something that has bothered me for years. As the cliché goes, I remember the night like it was yesterday. It was the mid-2000s. I was standing outside the Johannesburg City Hall smoking a cigarette with a friend, Zee.

There was a gala event to celebrate South Africa's literati, including the naming of Professor Keorapetse Kgositsile as South Africa's poet laureate. At the time, I was knee-deep in the poetry scene, although, looking back, my efforts in that space were not as significant as I thought, or would have liked. Probably because I didn't follow through on a lot of things, and life took over, but that's a story for another day.

On that night, for some reason, the legendary poet and writer, Don Mattera, came to stand with us. I did not know him too well and was not sure that he even knew who I was (who am I?), but he had interacted with Zee enough to warrant a conversation that turned, very quickly, into a lesson on poetry and life.

He talked about a tree. He talked about a tree as a metaphor for life. He talked about a tree as the root for poetry. He talked about how us young poets seemed to be so submerged in 'I' that our poetry always fell short, creatively. As he talked, my poems rang through my head, all launched by 'I' and 'I' served as my raison d'être. I tried to silently and mentally write a poem about a thought, a belief, a feeling, a concern that did not stem from 'I' but failed miserably. Fortunately, because the words were not being spoken out loud, my failure was not laid bare for him to see. Yet, it was.

Now here I sit, writing a whole book that is about me. Steve Biko said, 'I write what I like.' I can, and could, use that as an excuse, but I have never felt comfortable doing so.

Papa Don talked and we listened, without argument. Without explanation. Without excuse. We did not retort with theories of how our time needed us to voice the views of self as a voice for others because he has done that for years. With a tree as a metaphor for life, or joy, or pain, or thought, or feeling, he was talking craft and creativity and voice.

I often think back on that night when I write, not just poetry, which I don't write as much of as I did then. At some point, I decided that I had retired from poetry, although many have said one cannot retire from poetry. Funny thing is, all it took was time for those who knew me from that context to move on. When I first started at *Destiny Man*, I would get asked, 'How does a poet become an editor of a business and lifestyle magazine?' By the time I left the magazine, there were fewer people who saw me as a poet.

I could have saved myself many an argument with people who seemed to take offence at my 'un-labelling' myself, even though it was after many nights of climbing on and off open-mic poetry nights that I decided to label myself 'poet'. I figure, if I can decide I am a poet, I can decide I am not.

Anyway, writing for self seems to breed a narcissistic view to writing. We have so many avenues to share our opinions that we have become a world that places more value on the individual's opinion than the quality of thought that goes into forming that opinion.

When I was a magazine editor, I would often receive emails from writers who wanted to contribute, primarily in column form. One particular day, I received a phone call from a young man in Soweto, who wanted to write a column for *Destiny Man*. He started off well, telling me about how he loved the columns we already had, then veered off into how 'he had a story to tell' as a young South African man.

While I agreed with him that it was – and is – necessary to get a diversity of thought in the media, I had two challenges that I would need his help to deal with. The first was that, considering I received countless requests from young men, and women, who had stories to tell, how was I to decide who merited a column in the magazine. His view was that, since I had taken his call, it should be him over the others.

The second question was which columnist I should cancel to accommodate him because the simple reality was that there was only space in the magazine for four columns. I couldn't add a page so I would have to get rid of someone for him to replace. To this he had no answer.

A column is basically an individual's opinion, hopefully an insightful, thoughtful one. It had taken me a decade of writing for various publications and my own site about things that I would have preferred not to write about just to build enough of a reputation to be granted a column to share my views.

I acknowledge that I can be a bit cynical about the media world, especially when it comes to the writing side of things, but that's not the point of the story. The point is simply that it took many years of building a reputation as a writer to get to the point where I would be commissioned to write from the 'I' perspective.

And while I have built my career on writing about my experiences, I have also had to write about other people, putting a spotlight on their lives and their views. Hopefully, it is that work that allows me to be a little lazy and focus on storytelling that is rooted in 'I'.

I often think back to that night with Don Mattera. I wish I could take the valuable lessons he shared and apply them to my writing, even today. I do not have an answer as yet, so I keep asking and I keep writing.

Reading to write

READING ZADIE Smith's essays in her book *Changing My Mind*, which is about authors such as Nabokov, Eliot and Kafka, there was a question that bothered me. Can I consider myself a writer if I haven't read what some consider 'the classics'? While I enjoyed Smith's thoughts on these writers, I had little desire to actually read them. I have always tended to follow my 'gut' when it comes to what I read, without any real logic to it.

What are often considered the classics are frequently heavy, dense books in terms of language and thought, and I am rarely in the head space to tackle them. In high school, it took me three years to read Tolstoy's *War and Peace*, starting it several times before eventually getting to the end. I cannot tell you much about it now, so many years later, but, when I hear other writers talk of it, I wonder whether I read the same book. Hence, my comfort with rather reading Zadie Smith's writing on similar literature, which I do recognise is a cop-out; her essays serve as kind of crib notes for literary classics.

In a way, it is similar to lingering on the edges of other literary and social spaces, where, if one hasn't read any Fanon, for example, you continue to be on the edges, never quite belonging and are perceived as not intellectual enough by some. Is my excessive willingness to share the fact that I read Malcolm X's autobiography at an early age a manifestation of this inherent wish to be accepted within certain spaces?

My time in Joburg's poetry/spoken-word scene put me around enough tables where poets, writers and other activists talked up the works of people like Dambudzo Marechera, Chinua Achebe, Bessie Head, Ngũgĩ wa Thiong'o and Wole Soyinka. At times, it felt like a performance of sorts where who you have read validates your intellectualism and serves as a flag to be planted to reserve your space within the discourse. I have read James Baldwin, Alex La Guma, the aforementioned Achebe, Ayi Kwei Armah, amongst others. I fell in love with Richard Wright's *Native Son*, Ralph Ellison's *Invisible Man* and the poetry of Amiri Baraka and Don Mattera as a teenager, but all of this was because they were available on the shelves of my father's library and I enjoyed the writing. They were never symbolling. Perhaps that is my downfall.

I read as a form of escape. I read for the enjoyment. Sometimes I read to be a better writer. Reading to become a better writer is necessary. However, what if one is a reader that does not absorb every word or gets distracted by each turn of phrase rather than retain the elements that either reinforce one's ideas or take the reader on a journey that focuses on the destination of that particular piece of writing? And what if the end is merely another station, in another town, which one needs to explore before carrying on? It's all very complicated. Perhaps that is the purpose: reading as an act of shining a light on the shadows in one's own thinking in a way that is introspective and outward looking, at the same time.

I find myself in a weird space, trying to find the point of overlap between me as a reader and me as a writer. I have written business proposals and reports. I have written television concepts. I have written scripts for television. I have written poetry. I have written extensively for magazines. Writing is a muscle that needs to be constantly and regularly flexed to build strength, yet the 'exercise' you do in one type of writing does not automatically carry over into others. Sometimes I skip writing's equivalent of leg day and end up with a top-heavy, spindly-legged writing body.

As Colin Nissan, writer for spaces such as *The New Yorker* and *The New York Times*, so wonderfully put it, 'Writing is a muscle. Smaller than a hamstring and slightly bigger than a bicep, and it needs to be exercised to get stronger. Think of your words as reps, your paragraphs as sets, your pages as daily workouts.'

There are two parts to this. Firstly, there is the craft. Finding new ways, and new words, to express. Navigating the labyrinth that is language and its rules – whichever language you write in – and finding ways to put the puzzle pieces that are words together in such a way as to best communicate whatever it is you want to share. The second part is understanding that each genre has its own 'tricks of the trade'. Writing for a magazine is very different to writing poems, writing for newspapers, writing press releases, writing proposals ... the list goes on. Which muscle do I work on and what do I read to better understand that muscle?

Perhaps the fear is that, in reading what many consider 'greats' in writing, I won't grasp the words beyond the words on the page, which can create doubt in my own ability or at least the quality of my thoughts. Yet, at the same time, it is important to tap into the wisdom and knowledge of those who have come before you, building on it and adding your own perspectives to the overall discourse.

Trying to remember

MEMORY IS a funny old thing. You tell a story so many times, you start to question how much of it actually happened. With each telling of the experience, you smooth out the edges, the things that didn't quite fit in, to the point where you can tell it at the drop of a hat.

When I started performing poetry, I had to learn the craft of standing on a stage in front of people, who would, generally, get increasingly tipsy as the night went on. In the late 1990s and early 2000s, open mics were notorious for running longer than they should have. Poetry is great, but, after the third hour, it all starts to blur. I had to learn mic control, rhythm, tempo and even tone to keep the audience engaged.

By the time you have both memorised and performed a poem over ten times, all of that becomes second nature – where to speed up, where to slow down, when to raise your voice, when to bring it down to a whisper. I can take a poem that I haven't performed in years and fall comfortably into its voice, like putting on a well-worn pair of shoes or jeans. Even when I want to mix things up and try something new with the same words, I end up in the same place.

It's similar with the retelling of memories. It becomes automatic. You learn how to build up to the punchline or moral of the experience.

In 2014, I had the opportunity to travel to Los Angeles with the whiskey brand Jameson, which ran a film competition open to South Africans, Russians and Americans. The winners from each country had the opportunity to shoot a short film over three days with the production company Trigger Street Productions, formed by Kevin Spacey. Every year, there was a different A-list actor to feature in all the films shot – that year was Uma Thurman.

Part of the trip was the opportunity to interview Kevin Spacey – before his star started to fade following repeated sexual assault allegations. I was there representing *Destiny Man*, there was someone from *GQ South Africa* and a couple of bloggers. We all had ten minutes with Kevin Spacey.

It is one thing to know that actors at that level of the Hollywood machine have been interviewed ad nauseam over the years, but it is another to experience what that means first-hand. Spacey was so polished, he essentially told each of us the same story, word for word. A whole thing about when you get to the top, it's important to send the elevator down.

While I was mildly indignant at the time, having to write an article that was different, yet from the same information that had been given to others, looking back, I realised that I do the same thing with interviews. Repeat the same stories, word for word. With hindsight, we subconsciously add bits and pieces to ensure that the retelling is designed for maximum impact and, as a result, it becomes a performance.

This makes the process of reaching back through my lifetime challenging yet interesting, reflecting on how the different experiences influenced me and taught me lessons: having to scratch deeper beneath the surface over and over again until one gets to the heart of things. But there is always the risk of grabbing onto something that didn't quite happen.

Attempts at being an actor

THE LESSONS sometimes come from the most unlikely places and one of those places, for me, was the process of trying to get into acting. I have never enjoyed the spotlight and, in my younger years, when the spotlight was on me, I would withdraw within myself. I would seek the safe places in my conscious mind, face stoic, hiding the turmoil going on just beneath the surface of my skin.

I used to have pictures of the French Foreign Legion on my wall in high school. They all had the same impenetrable expression on their faces. In the accompanying article, one of the soldiers said that to get the expression right, he would stare at himself in the mirror. I wanted to join the French Foreign Legion, go away for five years, get given a new name, no connection to the past, spend my days training and waiting for war. In preparation, I would practise staring at myself in the mirror. I would go further and experiment with it in class on my teachers. My one French teacher never knew whether I understood what was going on or not because I always had the same expression on my face, regardless.

Fast-forward to the late 1990s, Johannesburg. Joining an actor's agency was all the rage. The country was opening up. South African television was also expanding programming, especially when it came to soapies and drama series that didn't treat Black people like caricatures. The advertising industry was on the rise, with commercials that incorporated various races, in the spirit of what became the failed Rainbow Nation experiment.

It seemed easier to get onto television, even if you hadn't been trained in acting, singing or dancing. It felt like there was a space for raw talent.

And, if you got to feature in an ad, the money was really good. My cousin Pepsi was a television presenter and introduced me to the people at the actor's agency Contractors, where I signed up. I would go to audition after audition without getting any work for at least six months. I did eventually do two Castle beer ads, one for print and one for television. And then, there was the opportunity to get onto the soap opera *Generations*.

The casting director was someone who had been involved in the agency when I signed up. I had an in and was auditioning in front of someone I knew; this was going to be the break that would send me on my way. I got to her office, we chatted a bit and then she had me do my lines in front of the camera. From the puzzled look on her face, I could tell that I wasn't going to get the part. Her feedback to my agent was that, when the camera came on, I withdrew into myself.

A decade later and a friend who was a regular on *Generations* – again – called me to talk about a recurring role on the show that she reckoned I would be perfect for. Against my better judgement, I agreed to audition. She even spent fifteen minutes before the actual audition going through the lines with me. Needless to say, the audition went as well as my first one. She kept on saying, 'Don't act.' In my mind, all I could think was 'but this is acting'.

In a phone conversation a couple of days later, it was a little amusing listening to the confusion in my friend's voice as she tried to let me down easy. What she couldn't understand was why, considering the number of television interviews I had had up to the point, I was so bad. Fortunately, I had a better understanding of my strengths and weaknesses and, therefore, it didn't bother me as much as the first time.

I recognise that I am wired so tightly and try to be very conscious of what I say and do – that it is hard to be anyone else, other than myself. Doing interviews, I am being myself, talking about what I know; I don't even consider the cameras. I am having a conversation with someone about something I am comfortable talking about. When I had a radio show on Kaya FM, while it took me a while to get used to speaking into a microphone to nameless and faceless people, I still had control over what

I would share, and it was generally my opinions, which isn't hard for me.

Acting isn't for everyone. I later went on to work at Contractors as a booker and saw a stream of people who wanted to act, some of whom were naturally talented and made the effort to work on the craft, and some who weren't. I met people who had gone further and studied the art of acting and it showed in the work they did.

People forget about the craft when it comes to the arts. We have seen so many people flourish, without having studied, that we assume desire alone will take us to the pinnacle. I used to joke that there is probably a De Niro, Washington or Malkovich lurking beneath the surface, but I am not inclined to put in the necessary work. There are so many other things, starting with writing, that I would rather put my energy into.

We all have multiple talents and abilities that we are born with. Living is about deciding which ones to pursue, doing them wholeheartedly and being accepting of the consequences, positive or negative. I have met people who say they would have pursued something in the arts, but, because it doesn't pay well, they decided to become an accountant or lawyer or something similar. There is a melancholy to this, yet it is a choice they made. It was firmly in their hands. The way I see it, if everyone operated with the same logic, there would be no artists or, for that matter, no entertainers or sportspeople, or the like.

Success in those fields is less than guaranteed and the journey can be hard. There are those who, despite all the challenges, still decide to pursue it. There are those who decide that the potential pain isn't worth it and go down a different path. Acting is that for me: too painful a journey that I would rather not travel. And that's all right.

Contradictory selves

I have lived a thousand lives
I have danced with angels
And fenced with the devil
For my soul

I have sat at the feet of wise men
And lain in the arms of mothers
Who teach without words

I have been oppressor
Carving pain into the skin
Of those who turned to me for help

I have been martyr
Throwing myself onto the spear point
Of society's expectation at the expense
Of what I know to be right
And so I write

My history shall linger in the recesses of minds still finding their way
Though we don't read anymore
And the libraries crumble
I can only dream of a legacy borne out of my experience

They say the children are the future
Yet that future shall be derelict

Don't believe the hype!

KNOW YOUR worth. It is a little sad that this has become a rallying cry of sorts. It says a great deal about our society that we have to regularly remind each other and ourselves that we each have value, that we each have something to provide. And even if we aren't giving something, we have value because we exist.

In isiZulu, *sawubona* (I see you) is the standard form of greeting. It is such a simple yet powerful word. You are acknowledging the other person's existence. Growing up, the highest form of disrespect was not acknowledging someone's presence. If you walk up to two or more people, you greet everyone, even if you know you are only coming to speak to one of them.

Being raised with this outlook and related values have made navigating Joburg, dare I say, interesting, for lack of better word. With Maseru being a small city and with my father being who he was, I was never anonymous – even if people didn't know me, they knew of me. In the early years of my life in Joburg, I was able to maintain a certain level of anonymity, which suited me because I generally prefer operating behind the scenes, but that didn't last long. Becoming a performing poet and then operating in the media means that I have built a bit of a public profile over the last fifteen years.

Watching how that has evolved and people's reaction to me has been, at times, both humbling and off-putting. Before *Destiny Man*, for example, some of my close friends were musicians, actors, presenters and the like, which meant that, when I was out with them, the attention was generally on them. What would often happen is that they would introduce me to people repeatedly, with some people forgetting me, which meant that the next time we met that person, they would introduce me again. Eventually, I would actually walk off when I saw the person coming.

When I worked as a booker at the actor's agency Contractors in the early 2000s, I was interacting with a lot of young performers who were at the beginning of their careers. It was my job to phone them when they had auditions. In the years that followed, after I left and some went on to bigger careers in theatre, film and television, there were some who would not remember me when we met in social spaces.

When I worked in television production for Bonngoe Productions, where I was first a researcher and then a producer, some started to remember me, and when I became founding editor of *Blaque* magazine, a few more people did. It was when I became editor of *Destiny Man* magazine that all of a sudden multiple memories were properly jogged and a lot more people across different sectors became interested in my existence.

My job title, in essence, deemed me to be of value and so I was a good person to know. When I went for the *Destiny Man* interview, a positive for me at the time was having just over 1 000 followers on Twitter and being quite active on Facebook. In those days, I would sign up to every platform and app, just to see how it worked, and I had gone through a year of obsessive tweeting. For my employer, the fact that I already had a presence on social media could only help.

Plus, a significant part of my work as editor of what was a relatively new title was to build its profile, so I spent a lot of time attending events and talking about the publication.

Public Enemy released the song 'Don't Believe the Hype!' in 1998. It spoke of not getting blinded by the 'smoke and mirrors' and was specifically targeted at a number of media people. It became a mantra of mine. In response to those who felt that it was awesome that I would be invited to everything from the opening of an envelope to a trip across the world and would be given all kinds of goodies, I would joke that 'my job title gets invited, and unfortunately, I have to go along'.

We place too much value on our job titles. Throw social media into the mix and it gets even more complicated. Peer recommendations became the thing. We woke up one day and started giving more credence to the recommendations of our peers than the marketing messages of brands. Brands realised this and started interacting directly with us and our peers. Some of us found that a larger community resonated with us, the things we said, the things we liked, and our follower numbers went up.

And that has become how we value everything. There was a time when we reacted to music on the basis of the music. Now, we talk about the number of streams and downloads in a song or album's (do people still make those?) first, second, third week. When it is announced that someone is now a billionaire, we rejoice and measure his or her value on the basis of that, as opposed to what they have done. Brands look at social media followers and negotiate with influencers on that basis.

This is all hype. It's important not to get caught up in this hype. If your value is rooted in it, it becomes a hard road when someone decides that you aren't that valuable any more because your followers have dropped, or you aren't increasing enough, or your engagement figures are low or your followers aren't of the best 'quality', whatever that means.

Leaving *Destiny Man*, I knew it was coming but not how quickly it came. Within two weeks of the announcement that I was leaving, my invites dropped by over 80 per cent. It was bliss. I was no longer useful because I no longer had the fancy job title. I could no longer 'amplify' their message.

I was always very clear to compartmentalise the two roles – the role of Kojo Baffoe, editor of *Destiny Man*, and Kojo Baffoe, the human being. I am the sum of all my parts and that is what I bring to any job that I do; the job is simply a job, regardless of the perceived importance of the title attached to it. All of that is just hype, which I try not to buy into because it is often fleeting. It changes at the whim of those who are placing value on it and it goes as quickly, if not quicker, than it actually came.

Find your lane

A MENTOR of mine used to constantly reprimand me about the potpourri of things that I involve myself in. According to him, I needed to pick an area, a specialisation, and focus on that, discarding any and everything that wasn't in line with that field. This is extremely difficult for me. It was then and it is now. My father designed my degree for me to be able explore multiple areas. Having majored in Economics, Marketing and Business Administration, business principles are business principles and can, therefore, be applied to different industries and sectors. That was, and is, the thread that runs through a lot of what I do.

I am a big proponent of 'finding your lane' and what I mean by lane can't be reduced to a single profession or a single specialisation. It is about finding the thread that runs through and binds everything.

For example, writing is something that I have always done, whether it was compositions in high school, poetry for my girlfriend, business proposals and reports for the family business or articles for our newspaper, and later magazines. I wrote proposals for my IT company, for the fashion designer I was working with, for poetry nights I was looking to host, and for television production companies. I consider myself 'a working writer' and, over the last few years, I have shifted from freelancing for magazines to writing for businesses, as they try to navigate this world of 'content'.

The focus, for most, is on the writing, and I have come to realise that what I do is not just writing but articulating ideas, thoughts and concepts. When I was writing for television, the few clients I had would come with the basics of an idea for a television show, which I would flesh out, translating the idea into a document that would hopefully allow the powers that be to see the images we had in our heads.

The quality of the thought is important but just as important is the ability to share that thought. When Twitter started, I loved that it forced you to be clear and succinct with your thoughts in 140 and then later in 280 characters. Even a thread needs to unravel in a way that is easy to understand. This is a skill many still lack, evident from the amount of conflict on social media due to tone and the inability to articulate thoughts and perspectives.

When I worked at *Destiny Man*, my mentor finally got it. I needed a working knowledge of a range of subjects to be able to effectively edit a men's business and lifestyle magazine. I didn't need to be an expert on each one, but I did need to know enough to both brief writers and know when an article was off the mark.

This has forced me to constantly engage with a wide range of topics and delve into the human experience to ensure that I can share thoughts and ideas in a way that is clear. What's my lane? I am a storyteller. I have, therefore, spent years trying to understand the different mediums available to me. It is a web and each space has particular boundaries, but, at the end of the day, the message/story should always be the same.

We have been going through a disposable stories phase, especially on the internet. Clickbait, 'how to' lists, catchy headlines, keywords and search engine optimisation are some of the tools of the trade. I came to accept that it wasn't my lane and, therefore, I would not get the attention that others may garner and the spoils that come with that. I could probably do it, but it just doesn't fit in with how I am trying to live my life and manifest my craft.

I have found my lane, for better and for worse. Coming to terms with this has been one of the hardest things to do, although it does make the journey so much easier when I let that understanding serve as the lens through which I see and engage with the world around me.

Curiosity and learning

THE QUOTE by Alvin Toffler, author of the book *Future Shock*, that 'the illiterate of the 21st century will not be those who cannot read and write, but those who cannot learn, unlearn, and relearn' has done the rounds extensively over the years, particularly as the world changes exponentially. The developments that the Information Age have wrought have forced us to question everything: work, education, socialisation, business and government. We need to revisit every nook and cranny, trying to plan for a future that is unknown and uncertain.

For years, we knew that what we learned in school only took us so far, but this has become even more so in the last ten to fifteen years. When my son talks about university, I often tell him that we do not know whether he will go to university because he still needs to decide what he wants to do after school. At some stage, he wanted to be a game developer, which I explained is something he could already work towards in primary and high school, since there are many resources available online for him to learn how to code. Plus, at his school, children start with coding and robotics from the age of five.

The one thing I try to emphasise is that what we learn in school is merely a foundation, a starting point from which we can launch into anything. What you learn at any given time may be the basics or may become obsolete as time progresses and more information becomes available. You have to allow yourself to learn, to be curious.

Sometimes, you need to follow the rabbit down the rabbit hole, instead of just standing on the edge and saying the rabbit went down the hole.

How deep does the hole go? How many rabbits are there? Is the hole in a park or on the side of the road? What's the neighbourhood like? Who lives in that neighbourhood? What are their hopes and dreams? How do they feel about the rabbits? Who has great recipes for rabbit stew?

I am often amused by the randomness of my life. How I have been able to make sense of that randomness is with a little curiosity and constant learning. The perfect example was working on a public franchising project at the South African Post Office in 2004. I was brought on as a communications specialist, but, three days into the project, the project manager pulled out and I was then made project manager. Estelle was working at the Gordon Institute of Business Studies (GIBS), giving me access to their library. I spent about a month poring over project management textbooks and developed reporting templates and task lists from these, taking into consideration the uniqueness of the project and drawing from the expertise of different team members.

Now we have Google and a digital universe with information on just about everything in the world. An important skill to have is the ability to search for information as well as how to be discerning.

Over the years, I have done this extensively and it has been a handy skill to have, particularly when one has to interview people from a wide range of sectors, disciplines and professions, for radio, for magazine and for digital platforms. My radio show, 'Life with Kojo Baffoe', on the Johannesburg-based station Kaya FM was essentially a show on anything I found interesting. I covered everything from fatherhood, renewable energy, watchmaking, poetry, philanthropy and music to Afrofuturism, archiving, art, cognac and cannabis. Every week, I would have to gather sufficient information and gain enough of an understanding of the topic to be able to ask questions that ensured that the listeners, and I, got answers that were insightful and informative.

I talked to an American blogger about a post he did on Beyoncé's sales funnel on how she uses different platforms, from performances to streaming services to Netflix, to share her creativity, crafting it in a way that speaks to everyone, from her hardcore fans to those on the fringes.

I talked to the ceramic artist Andile Dyalvane about how, through his work, he is actually archiving Xhosa history and culture.

I talked to young, Black tattoo artists about how they are tackling the challenge of working in a field that, at times, seems to go against cultural norms in South Africa.

I talked to African historians about how African history has been perverted and how they are going about changing that narrative by documenting and sharing the true history of Africa.

I talked to two conductors about the art and science of conducting orchestras and choirs, delving into how the job of conducting goes beyond the music and forces one to understand management and leadership, whether it is people (and their egos) or the business side of things.

Beyond this, I had to learn about the intricacies of radio itself, from running a desk and radio formats to editing audio and how interviewing live is very different from recorded interviews.

Curiosity takes you a long way and I never understand people who feel they know everything there is to know. In this rapidly changing world, it is important to have a base to work from, but I truly believe that it is as important to recognise that the base is merely a launchpad.

Let your work speak for itself

I HAVE grappled with the idea of a human being as a brand for years. I understand personal branding but feel that we have gone overboard because, for some, the focus has been the outward branding aspect instead of what the brand promises and its values – the substance of it. Many people seem to equate self-promotion with branding. Self-promotion, however necessary, has never been my forte, so perhaps my discomfort with human branding stems more from my self-perceived inadequacies than from the overall concept.

I am a human being, being human. Being human means doing the work. Being human means being part of a community, a society, and trying to live both in harmony and in a way that positively contributes. Being human means interacting with other human beings. It means living a life that you can be proud of. All of this means being conscious of how your words and actions impact on your life and the lives of others.

I operate on the premise that you should let your work speak for itself and speak for you. This is where I have always placed my attention. Less talk about what I am doing, what I am good at and why I think – or don't think – and more focus on actually doing stuff, to the best of my ability.

In my view, everything else is a bonus.

As a consequence, I have long come to terms with the reality that there have been opportunities that have passed me by because I have never been aggressive with 'marketing' myself. In a world where a human being's value is often measured by the number of followers, likes, comments and other forms of social media 'engagement', I have missed out on money that

I could have done with.

The way I am wired makes it hard for me to play that game; I view my value as a human being as being derived from the work I have done, the interactions I have had with people and the reputation, professionally and otherwise, that I have built over the duration of my life to date.

This is also probably influenced by my never having focused on building a career. My approach has always been simple. When something stops making sense in terms of the lifestyle I am building, I move on. When the next opportunity crops up, if it makes sense, I do it. I have learned to trust my intuition, my 'gut', as much as possible, regardless of how painful it may be. I have also learned how to walk away from things when they are uncomfortable, even, on occasion, when I have already agreed to do them.

I once got myself fired from a project because the effort it required was eventually more than the benefit. I had to disappoint a friend at the risk of losing that friendship, because the expectations were much more than I could deliver on, and it was making me miserable, which further impacted on my ability to perform. I must add that she understood even though it put her in a difficult situation. Also, I had attempted to find a replacement.

The only time I have ever had to really consider a career was not long before I turned 40. I had a session with a gentleman I had been referred to as a possible mentor and he honestly laid out the reality of my situation: I was reaching the age at which companies were not hiring unless it was for a senior position. And, considering I had not worked in the corporate environment at all, it would be difficult to get a senior position.

Essentially, he was saying that I was middle-aged and companies were looking to hire younger people. The decision I had to make was whether to keep on the path I was on, pursuing my own projects, or jumping into a corporate environment and working my way up the ladder. Obviously, I went my own way, although, if I am being honest, with you and myself, there were no businesses knocking down my door to get me in.

I try to keep things moving. I try not to become complacent and dogged in my ways. I try to continuously learn from every experience, do and be better. This I do for my peace of mind and for my loved ones. If others see this and can also gain from my experiences, that's great.

But I am also not going to expend unnecessary energy on promoting some idea of 'Brand Kojo'. And, who knows, perhaps that is my 'brand'; perhaps, one day, I will wake up and realise that this perspective is flawed. To date, I have no regrets about how I have chosen to live my life and what I focus my attention on, so I will continue to focus on my work speaking for itself.

Kind of famous

RECOGNITION. I can never seem to get used to it. Perhaps that's a good thing. Allowed to run rampant, the ego can thrive on it, to the point of destruction. It does only happen to me occasionally. Not so much that it can go to my head, but enough that I recognise that I am not always operating under the complete shadow of anonymity. It usually happens in such random places that make it difficult to find any type of related pattern.

The first time I remember it happening was at an off-the-beaten-path petrol station. I was running between meetings and stopped to buy something to drink and a pack of cigarettes. There were two young women chatting to the cashier when I walked up. One of them looked over as I handed over my purchases and asked, in typical South Africa fashion, 'Sorry, aren't you Kojo, the poet?'

It seems she had seen me sharing poetry at the Gordon Institute of Business Studies, where she had been part of the Spirit of Youth programme that Estelle was instrumental in setting up. A select group of high-school children from a range of schools came together once a month at the GIBS campus for an experiential programme. For a couple of years, I regularly performed poetry and spoke on race and identity.

I have famous friends. I am used to people around me being recognised. I am used to being the person politely greeted as a necessary inconvenience or being ignored totally. Even as my profile grew, especially when I was with *Destiny Man* and, later, Kaya FM, the nature of my work has never really been that sexy. I mean, I write stuff. It isn't as cool as being on telly or making music or something. On radio, I was on at night, once a week, talking about random stuff like philanthropy.

One of many lessons I learned from radio was that making assumptions about your audience was a surefire way of failing. I thought I knew who would listen to the show, and who wouldn't, and then discovered my audience ranged from cashiers to CEOs, waiters to doctors, artists to entrepreneurs. It was heartening to discover kindred spirits who are curious about the world.

When Kweku was four, I was dropping him off at kindergarten one morning when a teacher walked up and waved a page torn out of an old copy of the magazine *True Love*, with a column I had written accompanied by a profile picture. She showed it to Kweku, thinking he would be as excited as she was. He looked at it, said it was 'Daddy' nonchalantly and ran off to play with his friends. By this stage, he had seen me on TV a few times and was used to seeing my picture in a magazine. There were always copies of *Destiny Man* around the house.

Two years later, a primary-school friend of his who had seen me on television asked him whether his daddy was famous. He promptly came to ask me the same question. I gave him what had become my standard answer, which was that my work for a magazine meant that sometimes I would be in magazines, on radio or on television. As I walked away, I heard him shout to his friends, 'He's only a little famous.'

What does it mean to be famous? What is the significance of it? I have friends who are deemed famous or celebrity, but that has, or at least should have, no bearing on our relationship, should it? A friend once apologised for not reading *Destiny Man* because they weren't really interested in the content; I saw no reason for the apology. It was what I did to put food on the table and look after my family; my job was not me.

I do take pride in that, generally, when I am recognised, it is for my work as opposed to the places I go, the people I hang out with, what I wear or any of the other external criteria that some seem to focus on in determining a person's importance or value. While a little alarming, I do feel a sense of accomplishment when told that something I wrote or said had a positive impact on someone's life, however small.

Life can be complex and confusing. I too look to the experiences of others for insights into how to navigate some of these complexities. It is probably why I enjoy reading biographies and autobiographies. It is a little weird to discover that others look to me, sometimes, for the same, especially considering that I still feel I have a long way to go. At the same time, I do recognise that there is an inherent responsibility to living parts of your life in the public sphere, particularly with social media. Even for the kind-of-famous. You never know who is watching and how what they see influences their lives.

Worse than a white man

I DO not profess to be an expert on matters like Affirmative Action or its South African equivalent, Broad-Based Black Economic Empowerment (B-BBEE). I did have a friend who worked extensively in the space break it down for me at a time when, for the layperson, it seemed to be very much about changing the ownership of companies to give opportunity to those who had been what is termed 'previously disadvantaged' in South Africa. This was the mid-2000s.

I also had the perplexing experience of a big IT company looking to buy into the small IT consulting company I started with a South African friend in the late 1990s. If we sold, we would have been made directors in the larger company. This was puzzling because, in reality, our company, at the time, had only one client and was generating no revenue as we were just starting out. The hope was that the one client would put us on retainer, after having completed a small job for them. In fact, we had used the money made from that small job to register the business, rent an office and buy a printer.

What shifted my understanding of B-BBEE was learning that there are seven pillars, including ownership, namely:

- Ownership;
- Management control;
- Employment equity;
- Skills development;
- Preferential procurement;

- Enterprise development; and
- Socio-economic development (social responsibility).

While the attention seems to have been primarily on ownership, followed by management control, like with most things in life, the inadequacies stem from human beings being able to implement, and we just cannot be trusted. Ownership has enriched the few, while management control has often been merely window dressing, with Black South Africans being put in management positions without any type of power. I do acknowledge that there are exceptions to the rule, but I still view them as exceptions, although don't ask me for stats. I have none.

The thing I have struggled to get my head around is how more effort has not been put into skills development, preferential procurement and enterprise development, which carry weightings of 15 per cent, 20 per cent and 15 per cent respectively. I do believe that simply focusing on these would take organisations a long way in contributing to the levelling of the playing field for Black South Africa and I say this while being essentially 'worse than a white guy'.

There was a time when I would get approached to become part of companies or consortiums that were looking to bring colour to projects. Imagine the horror when it was discovered that, because I am a 'foreign African', I would dilute the B-BBEE score from an ownership and management control perspective! This puts me at the bottom of the proverbial food chain where a white South African male is considered to have more relevance than I do because at least he is South African.

Suddenly, the calls would stop, and I would not be invited to meetings any more. It is why, eventually, I would announce my 'foreignness' at the start of conversations and only request 5 per cent shareholding, or just get paid more upfront without ownership. I am yet to get a deal.

Despite this, I buy wholeheartedly into the principle of B-BBEE when looking at the business landscape in South Africa, even today. I have had to, and continue to, work hard to carve a space for myself within a country that is my home, but I also recognise the privilege that comes from my background and my relationships. Everyone close to me comes from a space of disadvantage in one form or another and, in some ways, my complexion does disadvantage me, but I still have greater privilege in terms of my position, my upbringing, what I have been exposed to and the mentors I have had outside of South Africa.

It always puts me in a weird position, arguing for something that I am not a part of, although I am a part of it because it is of concern to the community around me and, if they struggle to progress, I also do not progress. To live in a mansion while all around you people live shacks just doesn't seem right to me. But, sometimes, being a foreigner can get in the way of my progress, which is why I often work through my wife's company – yes, I do front.

BEING THERE

Father of the year

FATHERHOOD IS complex in a country where many of the men who sire children don't take responsibility and are absent. It can be confusing in a world where the role of the father is very much up in the air now that we recognise that it isn't just about being the provider and the disciplinarian. Sometimes, I do wish we could go back to those simpler times but also recognise that would be a regression and, while many of us turned out all right, we need to approach it with the understanding that our children are growing up in a different moment in time.

Traditionally, our world has been structured around milestone upon milestone. Crawl. Walk. Run. Babble. Words. Sentences. Conversation. Kindergarten. Primary school. High school. Tertiary. In the world of work, it is about climbing the corporate ladder or scaling one's business, earning more as we go. It is a very linear outlook when nothing about life is linear, including parenting.

Acknowledged, each birthday your child hits is a milestone. Moving to a new grade is a milestone. But every time you feel you have a handle on parenting, your child throws a curveball. Plus, you can't protect them from the curveballs that life will throw them. You cannot wish away the disappointments, missteps and tragedy that they will face in the same way that your parents could not prevent the experiences that you went through. These are all part of living and what makes us who we are today.

I once read somewhere that the most helpless you will feel as a parent is the first time your child has their heart broken. You cannot fix it and you cannot prevent it from happening.

I have, at various stages, been part of collectives of fathers, where we share our thoughts on fatherhood. The discussion in a WhatsApp group I was once part of turned to how you determine your success as a father and what the related criteria for this success are. One father expressed the view that he considered himself successful because he was providing for his children; how they turn out as human beings is of no concern to him. This flies totally in the face of how I view it and it created some tension in the group.

My perspective is greatly influenced by the evolution of my relationship with my own father. It took me to reach my thirties to recognise and acknowledge his success in raising me. The measure I use relates to how I have turned out. And I would like to think that I have done all right. Flaws and all, I try to do right by those around me, and I try to contribute positively to my community. I am not a serial killer. I am not evil. I constantly work at being the best version of me, using the tools that my father shared with me.

As to my scorecard as a father? My children will complete that when they are adults and can look back over the sum total of my words and actions. My success will be in the lives they lead, and whether they feel my guidance provided them with the tools to be the best versions of themselves.

Raising a boy and a girl

IN MY past lives, at least the ones that I have been able to tap into, I was a male. Yes, I believe that I have lived before. There was a psychic/tarot reader I had a session with once who unpacked a couple of my past lives, and drew a picture of one of my guides, a monk called Basilio.

It feels strange to say but I feel very much 'a man', whatever that means. This form feels like one that I have had previous experience with. Interestingly, I have heard it said that when you reincarnate as a woman, that's when you have reached the highest form of consciousness. It sounds about right.

I grew up in a male-dominated household, with my father and two brothers. My older sister was out of the house, at boarding school and university, more than she was in the house, so my younger sister was surrounded by males.

To say that we, my brothers and I, were oblivious to whatever challenges and transitions my sister went through is an understatement. It was only when I was older that I realised that my father had to, on occasion, deal with my sister's transition into womanhood and everything that comes with that, like periods and bras. At the time, it never occurred to me.

Having a son as my first-born was easy, from the serious to the trivial. When he was born and there was a discussion on circumcision, I dominated that and Estelle, to a certain extent, followed my lead. Later on, the discussion on body odour and adolescent boys was another that I was forthright about. I also went through those transitions and so I could – and can – speak from experience.

As one of my colleagues at *Destiny Man* used to say to me, when we were discussing story ideas, 'you have the tackle, so I follow your lead'.

Buying toys for a boy, especially one with similar interests, was easy. Then Ayanna came into my life. To start off with, I balked at the amount of pink that seemed to precede her arrival. Clothes, bed sheets, toys, basinets; everything for girls seemed to be in pink. I complained to anyone who would listen that there are other colours in the spectrum and why should everything for girls always be pink. The universe put me in check very quickly. My daughter's favourite colour for her first five years in the physical realm was pink.

To raise a child is no child's play. To raise a child in a world where patriarchy is so destructive is no walk in the park. It manifests overtly and subtly. Walk into a toy shop and the girl's section is often filled with dolls and doll houses, and toy household appliances. The science stuff tends to be closer to the boy's section. The language we use reinforces how society says girls should be versus how boys should be. Run like a girl, hit like a girl, cry like a girl: these all perpetuate the idea that girls and, by extension, women are weak or less than, with boys and men used as the yardstick or standard for anything and everything. The word we use for a girl who is physically active or dresses a particular way is 'tomboy'. That says a lot about what we consider appropriate for girls.

I continue to try to not reinforce these. It may seem trivial, but, while Kweku plays drums and Ayanna plays the piano, it was Ayanna who took to drums first and went to lessons for a year before she decided she wanted to play the piano. I try to encourage both of them to explore. The job of a parent is to expose our children to as much as possible and allow them to find the activities that resonate with them.

It is also about understanding their unique traits and helping them manifest these, while not blocking the things they enjoy, even if it is 'not in line' with their gender. I have had to learn this with Ayanna and it does help having Estelle on the journey with me. She serves as a great example. She is a professional who works hard but also enjoys life wholeheartedly and both Kweku and Ayanna see this. There has been many a time when she brings home the proverbial bacon, and she is a lot more decisive in situations where I may hang back. For example, she is very vocal when she doesn't receive the service she expects, while I tend to gloss over it. If we are in a restaurant, while she would voice her displeasure, I am more inclined to say nothing but never go back again.

Also, she is a woman, a feminine one at that, and this has taught me a great deal. It is changing, albeit slowly, but there have been times when a woman in the workplace, focused on her career, would suppress her femininity to get by, to not be intimidating to men by, to a certain extent, mirroring men in dress and demeanour. I guess what I am trying to teach both my children is that this shouldn't be normal. Ayanna shouldn't have to restrict herself and suppress parts of who she is and Kweku shouldn't expect, encourage or accept it when he is interacting with girls and women.

Ayanna likes so-called girly things – playing with dolls and make-up – and that is okay. At the same time, she's interested in robotics, gaming and painting. She should be able to embrace all of that. Kweku is a teenager now and is starting to pay more attention to how he looks, the clothes he wears and how his hair is styled. There's nothing wrong with that, either. He should be able to try anything without being told that boys don't do this, or boys don't do that.

As they grow up, there will be things that come to the fore that I probably haven't considered yet. For example, while I am aware of the reality that women menstruate, I had not thought about it in relation to Ayanna until an interaction I had with an initiative called The Pad Run, which seeks to provide young girls with sanitary products and menstruation education. They sent me a 'starter kit' of sorts for Ayanna. I slept fitfully the night before going through what I would say to her.

Fortunately, it is something that Estelle could talk through with her, but it is important for me that both Kweku and I form part of the conversation because, in truth, the negativity often comes from us as men and boys. We opened the 'Flow Box' together and reiterated how, firstly, there is nothing wrong with menstruation and, secondly, we are all there to support Ayanna.

I loved that Kweku was aware and that he did not have any type of misconceptions or negativity about it. I can only hope that he will be understanding and have much more empathy than I did at his age, being oblivious to the challenges that women face.

Overall, I don't always get it right, but I am constantly reflecting on my words and my deeds, considering what message I am passing onto my children. I want the same for both of them. I want them to be able to live full lives and experience as much of the good as possible. I want them to be able to explore all that is available to them. It isn't one type of thing for Kweku and another for Ayanna just because of the gender they were born with. Ayanna shouldn't have to live in a world that is uncomfortable, just because she is a girl (and eventually a woman) and Kweku shouldn't perpetuate all that is wrong with a patriarchal world.

Work on you

THIS IS one of my favourite quotes on children by Elizabeth Stone: 'Making the decision to have a child – it is momentous. It is to decide forever to have your heart go walking around outside your body.'

It doesn't seem possible until you have a child. And, when you have two, it becomes even more intense. When we are children, we talk about who is the favourite, who is loved more, etc. Now, I am sure that there are some who perhaps find it easy to have a preference when it comes to their children, but I am not one of those.

I love them each as intensely, just differently. Very early in my fatherhood journey, I realised that being a father is as much a process of self-discovery as it is of guidance.

A friend once said to me that the best advice he ever received about parenting was 'to live your life to the fullest'. Seeing you live wholeheartedly, your children will observe and understand that it is possible, even with your failures and missteps. If they see you get up, time and again, they will internalise that much more than you repeatedly telling them that when you fall, it is important to get up, dust yourself off and keep going forward.

My father did this with me in his own way. He would often say that eventually we would have offices for our multiple businesses – B&A Holdings, with its subsidiaries Baffoe & Associates, B&A Informatics, B&A Agencies and anything else we established – in Maseru, New York, London, etc. Although the businesses were small at the time, operating out of one office with a team of about ten people working across the different businesses, it never seemed far-fetched to me, not because he said it but because of how I saw him work daily. He travelled regularly, working on projects across borders, comfortable in any space. When something didn't succeed, he wouldn't sit around moping, he would put it behind him and look to the next thing.

With the birth of Kweku, I realised very quickly that it was necessary to work on me if I wanted to be a half-decent parent. I have always been a bit of an introvert, very comfortable in my own space, and in my own head. Sometimes a bit too comfortable. It is easy for me to check out and withdraw from the world. In the early days, when Kweku was one, I was working from home, spending hours alone in my home office, writing well into the witching hours. There was a period when, with hindsight, I realise I was physically present but not mentally.

My Aunt Pam calls it 'my fucking hermit tendencies' and it always jars me because one doesn't expect to hear such language from a sixty-plus-year-old African woman. I suspect that's why she puts it like that. It forces me to hear and not dismiss. I have learned to spot the signs better and have to work constantly on this tendency to be in the same house but drift away into my own world.

And this is only one aspect of my personality that I have to work on. I can nag, a trait that I got from my father, and, in the same way that it irked me when he did it, it irks my family. I can also blow my top quite quickly when something the kids have done displeases me. I recognise how this doesn't help any situation and I am trying to be calmer and gentler when reprimanding them. It isn't easy. I am a work in progress, as a man, as a husband and as a father. It is about understanding this and working on me constantly.

Presence over presents

I AM writing this during the extended lockdown caused by the COVID-19 pandemic that has changed the world, after about four months of being indoors with the family. We do lockdown relatively well. Its impact on work for Estelle and I has been potentially devastating, but we keep on, with an element of faith and belief in the universe, in our ability, in our commitment and conviction. We are fortunate to have a home where everyone has the space to be on their own when needed and we aren't on top of each other.

My routine did not change much during hard lockdown. Help the kids settle into schoolwork online, make a cup of coffee, put on some music, sit at my desk and journal. Following that, get into whatever work I had to do for the day, including writing for clients, blogging, pitching for work, etc. It is the basic routine that I have maintained following my departure from a full-time job at *Destiny Man* magazine in 2014.

One of the main reasons I left a job that for many seemed like the pinnacle of media work was because I was living a parallel life to my family. I travelled overseas once every month or two. I attended at least two evening events a week. I wrote in addition to editing. I attended multiple sales, editorial and management meetings. And, even when I was home, I was often catching up with my writing.

I had watched my father work himself to the bone. For years, I battled with insecurity around how much I worked because it never measured up to my father's level of workaholism. When I was in high school, he would get home from the office at around 7 pm, sit on the couch, have his supper and then fall asleep. After getting my younger siblings to bed, I would wake him up and send him to bed.

I never wanted that life for myself. He was a single father of five children (four in the house) and an entrepreneur, which meant he had to put in the extra work. I have always believed that it is my responsibility to provide my children with a foundation to build their lives that is a step up from the foundation that my father laid for me, as well as learning from him, including what he did that I wouldn't do.

He rarely, if ever, attended any of my school activities. He saw me run once and I had already left high school when that happened. He didn't have the time or energy to find out what was going on in my life.

For most of my high-school and university life, money was erratic. Having to ensure that we all had access to what we needed – food, clothing, education and shelter – while living the tenuous life of an entrepreneur was not always easy. You always had a sense of what the situation was from whether there was yoghurt and cheese in the fridge, which my father loved. Having been the one groomed from an early age to be involved in and eventually take over the family businesses, I generally knew a bit more about the realities than my siblings.

I never wanted that for my family. The idea of spending all my time working for my family but never really seeing them just didn't sit well with me. My presence was, and is, important to both me and hopefully my family. This, and discovering the concept of 'lifestyle design' from reading Tim Ferriss's *The 4-Hour Workweek*, are what prompted me to leave *Destiny Man*.

At the time, I wrote a blog post titled 'I Quit My Job for My Children'; interestingly enough, it became one of my most popular blog posts:

> It's an ordinary Monday, in that blurry space between autumn and winter, when the sun seems to beat a hasty retreat into alternate hemispheres. I am sitting on a beat-up plastic chair watching a boy – my son – go through non-stop drills at football practice, his orange football boots reflecting the fading sun's rays. Twice a week, most weeks, I sit watching my son at football practice. This particular Monday, when he is done, we hop into the car,

rush through to pick up his younger sister from kindergarten and head through to swimming lessons. And, at home, I sit with him as he does his homework. I believe that this is partly what being a father is about. Being available to my children.

Two years ago, my reality was very different. I was working in a fulfilling but high-pressure job that required me to be out constantly and involved regular travel. That year, I was attending about two events a week, writing articles constantly and doing about six international trips. I went to Germany – Stuttgart specifically – for one night, leaving on a Monday evening and landing back home on a Thursday morning. Dropping off my then seven-year-old son at school on the Monday morning, his response to my telling him I would be away was an extremely nonchalant, 'Okay, see you.' He was used to having Skype conversations with me from random hotel rooms. If I phoned instead, it wasn't uncommon for either of my children to not want to speak to me because they were too 'busy' to talk.

Even when I was home, in reality I wasn't because my mind was often on the work and trying to keep up on weekends, because there weren't enough hours in the day. And there were days when I just wanted to do nothing – watch football, vegetate, sleep – but there was never time. It's like walking off a plane at the height of summer in Accra; it is so humid even the air is heavy, making it hard to breath.

There are few things as disheartening as the moment when you realise that you are living a parallel life to your family, that they have their routine, their 'things' that go ahead with or without you. I was a visitor.

Being an adult isn't child's play. Eventually, something had to give and that something was my prestigious job as editor of a men's business and lifestyle magazine. Okay, there were two other considerations, but a large part of my decision was based on being a firm believer in the 'presence over presents' parenting approach.

It may have taken me over a year, but the day I walked away from the job and into my home office was the day I became happier. It was the first day when the weight that I was carrying – though I didn't realise I was carrying it – became lighter. It took me a couple of weeks to find a new rhythm – and for my children to get used to my being home all the time, especially when they got home from school. My work life hasn't become easier – building a new business never is. Being clearer on the fact that I work to be able to provide for my family, and myself, and making decisions, accordingly, has enhanced my day-to-day.

Even when I miss moments – like a rugby match, or a school event – it doesn't feel as bad because they know that I am there, as much as I can, all the other times.

I have a lot more control over my schedule and work commitments. I decide on the projects I want to get involved in, taking my children's schedules and lives into consideration. I make decisions on the basis of the lifestyle I am working to build for us as a family. This is all good. Malcolm X said, 'The future belongs to those who prepare for it today.' I prepare for it every day because my future involves being able to create a foundation for my children. That is the intention I work with, today. Tomorrow? We'll have to wait till then.

I am perfectly comfortable in my own space and very much a homebody. I don't socialise much and would generally only go out to events to 'make an appearance'. An extreme reduction in events meant that it was an adjustment for both Estelle and the kids. By and large, it was a positive adjustment, but, with time, I have since discovered that there is a downside.

For about three years, Estelle travelled regularly for work. In 2019, she was away for at least a week a month, and on one occasion, three weeks. While the house ran relatively well during those periods, as he edged closer to being a teenager, Kweku and I started clashing more. We are similar in personality and temperament, which probably doesn't help much, but things came to a head four months into lockdown.

I always remember my father and my wife telling me that I was too hard on him when he was much younger. I was, and am, the disciplinarian. The one who always checked schoolwork. The one who would battle with him while helping with homework.

There is a danger to presence over presents. Sometimes, being present too much has its own challenges. When I need true time alone, I jump on my motorcycle and ride nowhere, not so slowly, for an hour or two. It is just me and my thoughts beneath the helmet and the beauty of the open road. Or I go to my favourite cigar lounge, Pedro Portia, for what I call meditation – smoking and random conversation. My family don't get that, especially my children. Sometimes, we need space from each other. We need to have a life that is separate from the ones closest to us in order for relationships to thrive.

In one of his older comedy specials, American comedian and actor Chris Rock talked of how boredom and routine – paraphrasing – are the foundation of every marriage. Yes, he did get divorced, but, in my view, there is some truth to this. If anything, you need time to accumulate enough external stories to bring back home, while being home. I reckon it was about five years into my marriage when Estelle started responding to any story I wanted to tell with, 'Yeah, you told me that one already.'

How I interpreted what Rock said was, with routine, you go through the motions for a month or two, dealing with family, work, life – and when you reconnect, you have new stories. I am learning that it is the same with children, if not especially with children. And it isn't about you, it is about them creating their identity and finding their place in the world, without you constantly looking over their shoulder. A relationship can't exist on just shared memes and videos that you see online. They have to make their mistakes. They have to find, lose and find their groove, their rhythm. They cannot do that with you in their space constantly. And sometimes they just need or want presents.

Fathers are not superhuman

WE WEREN'T always able to do it because of his working hours, but there were times when we would go jogging together in our neighbourhood, Lower Florida, next to the Mohokare (Caledon) River, which forms the border between Lesotho and South Africa. When the water was low, it was like a private beach for all the kids on my street.

My father and I would run out the gate, straight up the short dirt road, take a right onto the tar road in front of the Chinese Embassy and run about a kilometre to a field that was called Polo Ground. I assume that, at some stage, polo used to be played there, but, by then, all that remained was a dilapidated clubhouse and a dirt road in an oval shape.

Years later, I would take my younger sister there for driving lessons. There would also be parties, especially around Christmas time, and it was one of the spots in Maseru where young couples would park for some quiet time.

My father would maintain a running tempo that ten-year-old me could keep up with until our street. The gravel road that our house was on was about 200 metres, sloping down to our fence where there was a small side gate. When we got to the top of the road, we would sprint that last stretch. My father always beat me. He was, as all fathers are for our first couple of years on the planet, superhuman. Strong. Intelligent. A man for whom nothing was impossible.

It was only after we moved to a new house and I turned fifteen that I beat him in a sprint.

Before that, there was an incident that highlighted his human-ness, although I only really processed it much later. It was the late 1970s. At the time, Lesotho was governed by the Basotho National Party, and Chief Leabua Jonathan was in power from 1965 – just before independence – until 1986, when he was overthrown by a military coup. His rule was said to be autocratic and my father was a victim of an element of that autocracy.

He would later tell me what happened. All I remember is that one night, my younger siblings' mother said we had to go to the hospital. I walked into the room and my father was sitting on the bed, bruised and with cotton swabs covering both of his eyes. He had been brutally beaten by soldiers, thrown into the back of a van and dumped outside the hospital. He had been trying to reason with the soldiers, who were arresting a lecturer friend of his.

The room felt as cold and dark as his vision was. I was afraid and confused. He eventually came out of hospital a few days later but had to wear spectacles for the rest of his life as a result.

That was the beginning of the cracks in the herculean armour that I had created in my mind about my father, although he maintained a semblance of it on our sprints.

As he, and I, grew older, the less perfect he became. As his body started to age, and the muscles became less defined, the more human he became, in my eyes.

The funny thing is jogging was also involved the first time my son saw me bleed. As a former sprinter, I have never enjoyed running distances longer than 400 metres. For one, although I am always thinking, I would get bored and every stitch and pain would be amplified. But, around 2010, I decided that I would start jogging.

It was a Saturday afternoon, and I went for a run around our neighbourhood. I was using the Nike app on my phone, with a special running playlist. It was the last stretch. I was running on gravel on the side of the road. My power song – Rage against the Machine's 'Killing in the Name' – kicked in. I lengthened my stride and tripped. It happened in slow motion. It was one of those falls that go viral on social media; fortunately, I was alone, as far as I could see. I fell over about 10 metres.

There was a newly erected palisade fence to my right, surrounding a new secondary school that had just been finished. I started to reach for the fence to break my fall, but, realising that I would probably cut my hand, I pulled it away at the last minute. Instead of using my hands to break my fall, I ended up using the side of my face and my right shoulder. I slid and rolled over, scraping my right cheek, my right shoulder and my knees.

I stood up quickly, dusted myself off, pulled some gravel from my cheekbone and knees, and phoned home to tell the missus. She wanted to know if she should fetch me, to which I replied in the negative and gingerly jogged the rest of the 800 metres home.

Estelle had decided to come fetch me anyway and I met up with her just as she was pulling out of the complex gate, with Kweku sitting in the back seat. When he saw the blood, he was wide-eyed and close to tears. I could recognise the moment. It was the moment that he realised that his father was not superhuman.

It is such an interesting dynamic and evolution discovering that one's father is flawed. It starts with the physical and, eventually, shifts into the mental. Realising that our father is also not the most intelligent person in the world and does not know everything is an even greater epiphany that comes with confusion and tension. You start pushing back more as a child, which, for a parent, can be extremely uncomfortable. It is easy to become defensive or to bully because, while the parent comes from a place of experience, not just 'book smarts', you, as the child, are still forming opinions, which haven't been lived through. So much of our world is relative and subjective, which complicates things even further.

I have had to learn to tell my children when I do not know something, which is not always easy. Nowadays, at least, we have Google so I can sometimes make it a teaching moment. But I would like to think that I know a lot, as my father also used to think. I am well read, have countless experiences to draw from, and I am constantly learning. Like his father and his grandfather, my son now thinks he knows a lot, and so we bump heads, especially since we also all want to have the last word. He hasn't learned to hold his tongue yet to appease his father. Perhaps it is a Baffoe trait. It took me a while too.

A lack of empathy

IT IS something that happens with some level of regularity. I hear the Angel (my nickname for Ayanna) crying and shouting at her brother. I shout my usual 'what's happening?' when the whining and arguing become too much. I walk into the room. The Angel says the Prince hit her. His response, 'I just tapped her.' For the umpteenth time, we have a conversation – more a reprimand – about how it isn't about you and how you feel someone else should experience your actions but rather about how the other person feels. A tap for me may feel like a hit for the other person.

In a way, it is easier to sympathise than to empathise. Empathy means putting yourself in the other person's shoes, so to speak, and trying to understand how, what and why they feel. Previously, it was believed that empathy was something that you are born with, but research has since determined that empathy can be taught. Plus, consensus is that narcissists are not born that way. It is a case of nurture as opposed to nature.

I think about this a lot when it comes to my children, and to teach them how to be empathetic means that I also have to learn how to be more empathetic myself. Too often, it feels like a lot of the challenges we face in the world stem from a lack of empathy. We operate with our own agendas; our interactions are driven by self-interest; and we feel our opinions are more valid. Don't agree? Spend a day on Twitter or Facebook and try convincing me otherwise.

So much conflict seems to stem from disagreement about how others feel and react to our own actions. We want to be able to dictate how that should manifest. We end up talking ad nauseam about how victims of racism, sexism, homophobia, etc. should react to things as opposed to tackling the root cause.

It is a painful and sad state of affairs. How we feel is real and should never be negated, but the world doesn't stop beyond our bodies and minds. With my children, I try to regularly remind them of how they would feel, and have felt, in similar situations when the proverbial shoe is on the other foot. So far, so good, but time will tell.

Finding themselves

ONE DAY, aged five, the Prince came home from school excited. He had decided that he was going to be a rock star and play the electric guitar. He handed me a flyer that had blazoned across it, in big letters, 'Do you want to be a rock star?'

His school had brought in a music academy to offer lessons and, on that day, they did a presentation for the kids. While the options were piano, guitar, drums and/or voice, as part of the presentation, the owner of the school had jumped on stage and ripped through a rock riff on the guitar, sealing it for Kweku. He insisted I attend an information session early on a Saturday morning. Once again, dude jumps on stage, gets down and dirty with the electric guitar, before giving background on the school, the teachers and the services. I have been around musicians and artists for years; he could not fool me with his rocking sales pitch.

Kweku had decided he wanted to be a rock star and play the electric guitar; what I felt had zero bearing on this. I probably should have taken an extended moment when they told me that he was too small to play an electric guitar and would have to start with an acoustic guitar. I phoned Kweku to tell him and, though disappointed, he said he still wanted to do guitar. Then the best part. He would need a guitar – a child's guitar – which cost a tidy sum, but, because they had our backs, they had discounted guitars for sale for that day only.

He was regular for a year and a half and then decided that he didn't want to play guitar any more. About a year later, both he and his sister wanted to play drums, so they started drumming lessons. The Angel got over drums and shifted to piano/keyboard. She needed her own keyboard, so I went out and bought one. The Prince, having kept up with drumming for at least a year, got a full drumkit.

Kweku had also played football off and on for about four years, the 'off' always seeming to come right after I had bought new football boots. And then there was rugby at school, which needed a gum guard, headgear and padding that he constantly outgrew. Rugby ended one year when he was stepped on in a game. Ayanna did gymnastics for about two years and, while she stuck with it for a bit, her enthusiasm also diminished. Both of them have been going to swimming lessons since they were two.

It may sound like I am complaining – I may be, just a bit – but, unfortunately for my bank balance, in my opinion, it is important to allow your children a multitude of experiences because, otherwise, how are they going to figure out what they like and don't like?

I can understand how parents end up spoiling their children when they have the means. It is a slippery slope because we all want what is best for our children and the line is smudged and blurry. In some ways, it feels worse in this world of abundance and advancement.

We spend each day working to build a foundation from which they can leap into the world and the goalposts keep getting shifted. We don't want our children to be left behind, yet there is no clear line delineating 'behind' and 'ahead' so we stumble our way through it, hoping that it all works out in the end.

We all grew up with a lack of, some time in our lives, and we turned out all right – well, some of us did, and 'all right' is also hard to define. One of the most difficult questions I have had to face as a father, and it is a question that I ask myself all the time, is: 'When do I say no, even when I am as capable of saying yes?'

As the cliché goes, 'There is no manual to being a parent.' What works with one child doesn't always work with the next one. What works with a child when they are five won't always work when they are six, let alone twelve years old. What worked today may not even work tomorrow.

This is encouraging and terrifying simultaneously. As they find what they like and don't like, you are also, like the drowning man, constantly grabbing at straws, flying by the seat of your pants. Even with repeated course correction, your child may feel you are being unnecessarily strict, unaccommodating or simply just mean.

And the 'do as I say' doesn't work as a catch-all for parenting any more, if it ever did. While there are clear boundaries, and I must confess I have on occasion used it, modelling the behaviour that you want your children to follow has become more salient.

If you want your children to have good manners, you need to have good manners. If you want your children to read more, or spend less time on devices, or clean up after themselves, then you need to read more, and have them see you read, and spend less time on your devices, and clean up after yourself.

Once you get beyond that, there is the challenge of them not doing as you do and the question of when to draw the line, because, perhaps, what it is you are doing may not be of interest to them.

What you feel is best for them is usually what they don't want in that moment. And let's be honest, we want to be liked and loved by our children. You want to please them, but you also have to lay out boundaries and stick to them, consistently. Fatherhood truly is a humbling experience.

For you

I speak these words for you
The centrepiece of my existence
The reason for each breath
Each step I take

I speak these words for you
On my tongue they glide like butterflies
Flitting between the beautiful colours
Of the world beyond the walls of my often grey-tinged mind

I speak these words for you
And wonder what I did before you

In my hazy memories
I glided through life, adrift
The fleeting moments of clarity
Gave me hope
They carried me through life's cacophony
In search of something
Anything to give me the direction
And the fortitude
And the focus
Needed to live with purpose
And legacy

Until you
And your brother

And then everything made sense

I have purpose now

And so I speak
And live
These words
For you

Street kids

ESTELLE GREW up in Parkside in East London, a residential area that was classified as Coloured. The family lived, and continues to live, in two houses across the road from each other. It was, and is, the type of neighbourhood where you always find children playing on the street outside. The neighbourhoods I grew up in were the same. Every day, after school, you would hear the sound of children playing, laughing, riding their bicycles, climbing trees and everything else that children do to occupy their free time when adults aren't bothering them.

We draw from those experiences in parenting our children but have also been confronted with how different the environment is that they are growing up in compared to ours. When Kweku was born, we lived in a two-bedroom townhouse in a big complex of more than 130 units, including apartments and a church. Just after he turned one, we moved to a bigger unit in a smaller complex. We had a decent-sized garden with a pool as well as a larger pool area with a squash court and jungle gym for the kids in the complex. Security was tight and Kweku would head out of our gate and stay away for hours without us being worried. The kids would be outside riding their bikes, playing football or just hanging out. They would be in and out of different homes, without any issues, just as Estelle and I experienced when we were growing up.

Once Ayanna turned six and was ready to go to the 'big school' her brother was already attending, we moved to a stand-alone house closer to the kids' school. I thought they would be excited; bigger rooms, bigger garden, big pool, bigger everything. Even after three years in the new place, they would still grumble about wanting to go back to the old place.

It is hard to blame them considering how their lives changed. Safety and security are a greater concern. The way people drive in the suburbs is very different from how they drive in a complex. You don't build the same relationships that you do in a complex. If the kids want to hang out with their friends, we have to drive them there or their friends have to be driven to our place. We live behind typical Joburg high walls with electric fences and, if they want to go outside the garden, an adult must accompany them. Kweku learned how to ride a bicycle in the safety of the complex. Ayanna's lessons need to be on the street amidst all the potential hazards. And, if they want to go riding, someone needs to be with them. There is no room for spontaneity.

It becomes complicated because in order to avoid them spending hours indoors, on devices or in front of the television, one has to be available to accompany them to go out and about. And although we are only a ten-minute walk away, I don't feel comfortable with them walking to and from school on their own. Kweku is reaching the age where he can and does occasionally, but to foist the responsibility of his sister on him would not be fair, and so they are dropped off and picked up daily.

While I want them to enjoy some of the experiences both Estelle and I had growing up, and while I want them to have some independence, the environment they are growing up is unfortunately very different. Neither of us has ever experienced a school being locked down because a child was missing from class. Our parents never received notices from the school with descriptions of an adult lurking around the car park trying to get children to go for a drive with them.

Sometimes, I wonder whether I am babying my children, but then I read another tragic headline and decide, if that's the case, so be it.

New-age children

'DADDY, DO we have electricity at home?' was the first thing five-year-old Kweku asked, jumping into the car after school one day. This was when there was regular load-shedding occurring across South Africa; well, one of the times, since this is something that happens relatively regularly. Load-shedding is when the electricity regulator, Eskom, shuts down electricity across neighbourhoods to relieve the load on the grid.

When I told him that we were load-shedding, his immediate reaction was, 'So, no WiFi.' When I was five, we didn't even have a television in the house. Our first TV in the early 1980s was followed by a Betamax video machine. The TV didn't even have a remote; one of us kids served as the remote when my father wanted to flip through the four channels that were available. Being the tech expert in the house in those days meant knowing which cables to connect and which channel to switch to when you wanted to watch a video.

My father started his business with a typewriter, upgrading to an electric typewriter and then, in my late teens, an Amstrad computer. I remember my first cellphone. I was in my early twenties. It was a Nokia 2110, a mobile phone in the true sense of the word. It just meant I could make phone calls on the move. When SMS became available, there was a limit on the number of characters.

I recall going onto the internet for the first time, with dial-up, the modem screeching rhythmically as it desperately reached out for the connection. My computer had a floppy disk for storing information.

I remember typing up and editing my father's documents with early word-processing software. To make a correction on page 68, you would have to scroll through every page. It meant being meticulous and paying attention, otherwise you would spend the bulk of your time scrolling through pages to fix spelling mistakes.

With the exponential evolution of technology, particularly in the last fifteen years, the world that my children were born into and are growing up in is very different from mine. The first time Kweku interacted with an iPad, he was two. Ayanna, at two, was happily and comfortably swiping through the same iPad. While conducting energy through a potato to power up a light bulb was cutting edge for me, they are contending with smartphones, satellites, WiFi, laptops, gaming consoles, tablets and smart devices.

They started studying robotics and coding early, as part of the school curriculum, and have been playing with music, design and other apps for years. We are getting to the point where, even with my relatively extensive knowledge of technology, they sometimes have to explain things to me, such as TikTok. When I bought them tablets, I spent hours setting them up in order to restrict and monitor screen time. Now they know how to bypass that, especially Kweku, in ways that I still don't understand.

It is such a weird place to be. I don't want them to be left behind so I expose them to technology as much as I can, but, with the sheer volume of tech advancements, it is near impossible to keep up. At the same time, they are being exposed to so much of the world's ugliness from such an early age and so I try to protect them while still trying to figure it all out.

I have realised that I can't block everything and, therefore, how I raise them is as important. For example, when Kweku had the picture of a rapper who had recently been killed as his WhatsApp profile picture, we had a conversation about how said rapper had been arrested for kidnapping and violence towards women. I asked him if he wanted to be associated with such an individual. As a then eleven-year-old, it was too much for him to grasp and I suspect he eventually changed the picture just because I disapproved.

Also, when he got a smartphone, the deal was that his mother or I could look through the phone any time we wanted to. And there have been occasions when what we have seen has prompted discussion. In a WhatsApp chat with his friends, someone remarked 'that's so gay'. I pointed out to him how close friends of ours – people he calls Uncle – are gay and how someone being gay or straight should have no bearing on the relationship with them. I added that, if one of his friends – or even he – was gay and perhaps trying to make sense of it, and they were part of that chat, they wouldn't feel comfortable being themselves with their friends, which is a painful place to be.

What our children are exposed to is so vast and diverse that it is impossible to protect them from it all. Plus, there are many positives that have an impact on how they view the world, people and their place in it all. Policing them and their interaction with technology isn't feasible. It needs to be coupled with providing them with the necessary emotional and mental tools to make sense of it. It is about allowing them the space to find the answers while cocooning them, as much as possible, from the negativity and divisiveness that form such a significant portion of our world.

What do you speak?

WHEN MY first nephew, Rendani, was born, I used to give my older sister, Grace, and my brother-in-law, Sandani, a hard time about not teaching him an African language, in their case Twi, Sesotho or Tshivenda. Sandani is from Venda. They would laugh me off and move on.

Estelle and I speak English. That's our common language and, by and large, my first language. That's primarily what we spoke at home growing up. I have read many articles on how to raise a bilingual or multilingual child and the common exercise is for one parent to speak to the child in one language and the other parent to speak to the child in the second language.

This meant that I would need to speak to Kweku in Sesotho and Estelle would speak to him in English. This was a challenge. I am most comfortable speaking English. While I would speak Sesotho to him in phrases, I believe that an important component of learning a language is hearing it spoken around you regularly. For about two years, from two to four for Kweku, we had a nanny/helper who was Mosotho, so she and I spoke Sesotho in the house. The minute she left, it was back to just English.

If there is one thing that being a parent has taught me, it is that while there are many things that work wonderfully in theory, when it comes to raising children, the practice is a whole different ball game. I feel that marriage and having children are the two things in life that you have to actually experience to be in a position to effectively contribute to the discourse. Many theories of the theories I had were simply that, theories.

Where does that put me in terms of language? Exactly where my older sister was. My children speak predominantly English. They both learned Afrikaans and isiZulu for their first three years in primary school. They are both doing isiZulu as their second language now. Would I like them to speak Sesotho? Yes. In the same way that I have been able to navigate the world without speaking any Ghanaian languages and speaking very poor German, they too will have to find their way.

There may be feelings of inadequacy that come with it, as I have had, especially when in Ghana or engaging with Ghanaians, but that's my journey to make sense of, just as they will have to do the same.

I will continue to try to expose them to multiple languages, because I buy into the whole concept of how bilingualism or multilingualism improve cognitive function; until then, sadly, it will be English as the predominant status quo.

The first time

THE PRECEDENT we set lays the foundation for how we move forward and yet we spend little time actually thinking about this. When you set a precedent that is out of sync with who you are, you end up spending unnecessary energy trying to maintain something that isn't you. I haven't been single for some years now but found the whole 'courtship' thing rife with pitfalls. My approach was to be myself as much as possible to ensure that, if that wasn't what was wanted, we could both move on without wasting too much of each other's time. I must confess that there were times when I set the bar low enough that the only way to go was up. Of course, this did take trial and error and time for me to mature enough to be comfortable with nothing coming of an interest or an attraction. Plus, all I had was my personality, because money definitely wasn't there for me to use as an added dimension.

Growing up in Maseru also probably helped because, while I did have a car before most of my friends, our lives and our circumstances were evident for all to see. We used to joke that all we had was the gift of the gab. When you are walking a girl to the taxi or you are all piling into a bakkie, ten deep, to go to a party, material possessions are inconsequential. What's important is your ability to talk, to state your case.

When Estelle and I started getting serious, I wasn't working, hustling small jobs here and there. A year before we got married, I ended up living out of a suitcase that stayed in the boot of my car, moving between her place, a friend's place and home in Maseru. I had been sharing a house with a friend, who I was also in business with. He left to go to the US – where he's from – for a visit. A few days after he left, we were evicted from the house, and I had to scramble to get my stuff off the side of the road and into Estelle's garage.

I was eventually able to get a job as a booker at the actor's agency, Contractors, and when Estelle and I eventually moved in together, my monthly salary only covered my half of the rent. For extra cash, I would do poetry performances and whatever else I could get my hands on. Sometimes, it would just be for petrol money for me to take her to work and pick her up at the end of the day. That's who she married. Trying to hide that from her would have been foolish, but I have seen people go to the ends of the earth to be seen to live a lifestyle that is way beyond their means.

When it comes to understanding the importance of precedent, becoming a father solidified it. I learned very quickly that when you say yes to something, a child's expectation is that the answer will always be yes. As they get older, you can reason with them, but I am still trying to figure out at what stage they start to fully understand or agree with your reasoning.

Today they ask, 'Daddy, can I jump off the ledge into the pool?' You say yes. Tomorrow, they don't ask, just jump. Perhaps you said yes because you were distracted and afterwards you realised how high and slippery the ledge is and medical aid isn't paid up so you can't be rushing to the hospital all willy-nilly. By then, it's too late because you said yes, without clarification, and now you are the indecisive one.

I had to learn to take a moment to really think the request through before responding. Also, because I didn't want to be predictable, I came up with the 'keep-them-guessing' technique to parenting. Sometimes I say yes and sometimes I say no. Sometimes I say no to something I had previously said yes to. Sometimes I say yes three times and then no once. Sometimes, in response to the statement and question, 'I know you are going to say no but ...', I say, 'Well, since you know I am going to say no, why ask?' Other times, I say, 'I was actually going to say yes, but let's work with your expected no.' And sometimes I just say yes.

By the time my children read this book, we should be beyond this phase, so I am not too worried about sharing this. Just don't tell them before, please.

Consistency is also important. Children do need boundaries. The way I see it, we shouldn't be too predictable in everything. We should consistently love them, be there for them and support them. They should know that we will always do what we feel is best for them and in their interests, even when they don't see it that way, but, with other things, unpredictability keeps them on their toes.

Be there, always

KWEKU HAD gone to visit a friend. Estelle was away on business in Rwanda. When I was dropping him off, he insisted that he was going to spend the night; he had even taken a bag with a change of clothes. We were close to the family; Kweku and his friend had been friends for about eight years, having bonded at crèche when they were two and moving to the same primary school together.

Later that night, I was attending a press launch when my phone rang. It was Kweku. He had decided that he didn't want to spend the night any more and wanted to come home. I told him that I was at an event and wouldn't be able to fetch him at that time and would fetch him first thing in the morning. He said okay.

About two hours later, I was catching up with some friends at a cigar lounge when I got a call from Estelle. He had been messaging her to say he wanted to come home. I chatted with his friend's father, who volunteered to drop him off at home. This was now after 10 pm.

Estelle and I were out for dinner at a friend's place. Ayanna was spending the night at her friend's house a street away from our home. This was a friend whose home she spends a great deal of time at. She messaged me from her iPad to ask what time we would be picking her up in the morning. She wanted me to fetch her at 5 am and, when I said it was too early, she disagreed vehemently.

At the same time, she was messaging Estelle and seemed fine when Estelle said she would pick her up at 9 am, but, in her messages to me,

9 am was too late. I told her that it made better sense for us to fetch her that night on our way home because the 5 am thing wasn't happening. She agreed.

Her last message to me was that she would probably be asleep when we got there – it was 11 pm – and I should carry her to the car. I tried to call her friend's father, but his phone was off so when we got to their house, I rang the doorbell, explained that she wanted to go home and carried her to the car as she was asleep.

Estelle and I had a conversation about where to draw the line in instances such as these. I want my children to know that they can call at any time when they feel uncomfortable or simply want to come home. I don't want them to ever feel like I won't be there for them, even if it might come with a mini-lecture later on. I would rather be taken advantage of than force them to have to deal with uncomfortable circumstances simply because they were more afraid of the consequences of calling me.

Trying to conceive

LATE IN 2001, I was kind of single, in the early stages of what had the potential to be a serious relationship with a young woman. We had been friends for about two years and, in the last few months, the relationship had taken a turn for the serious. It was a gradual process that evolved without pressure or expectation but rather as a natural transition. It didn't hurt that, due to accommodation difficulties, most of my possessions were in her garage and I, on occasion, slept at her place. We were 'going with the flow' and everything was going swimmingly until ...

One weekend, I went home to Lesotho to spend some time with family and get a home-cooked meal. Sometime during that weekend, we discovered – well, she discovered and then passed on the information – that she was pregnant.

I was 29 years old and a little broody – yes, it happens to men as well. This was not a train smash. We were two adults with the capacity to love and raise a child. It was not going to be easy, but I looked forward to it. I figured that if we were still together after the child was born, we could then consider the idea of marriage. It was not part of the initial equation. It was more important to plan how to create a loving home for this child who was going to come into the world. I had not been working solidly for about a year, so I also needed to make some key decisions to prepare myself. We made arrangements to move in together as we got closer to the time and we continued with our relationship.

A couple of months later, having thought things through and after a session with my then counsellor and friend, I decided that marriage might be a good thing and proposed. The pregnancy was difficult. It was ectopic and then it wasn't. The baby was underdeveloped, and everything was very touch and go.

I was going through an interesting phase in my life then. I had started working at Contractors. My boss and friend was involved in a great deal of spiritual work, including shamanism, reiki and tarot, which I began to embrace, including consultations with a tarot reader, who I still see to this day. I was attuned for reiki and would attend talks, sweat lodges and other related experiences, including an eight-month inner-child programme. There is an amazing man called Lionel Berman, who used to run talks and do readings. There was a two-month wait to get an appointment with him. During the early stages of the pregnancy, I was able to get in to see Lionel and some of what he shared with me served as great comfort. In essence, he said that since my mother had passed, her spirit hadn't returned to the physical realm as she was watching over myself and my father. She now felt that it was time and was returning as my baby, so, in a way, the baby represented my mother.

By the time we got married in June 2002, it had been seven months since we'd discovered Estelle was pregnant, but Estelle didn't look pregnant. One day, in August, Estelle called me at work to say she was going to the clinic to get checked because she was getting severe stomach pains. I couldn't leave work, plus it seemed a routine check-up. Sadly, that was as far from what it was as you can get. To be called by your wife telling you that she's had a miscarriage is painfully surreal. I still remember sitting on the phone, not knowing how to react and then rushing through to pick Estelle up and not knowing what to say. This was an experience that we went through as a couple but also individually.

In a strange way, I took comfort in that the pending arrival of my daughter Alaqua was the catalyst to recognising that I wanted to marry Estelle. I was fortunate enough to be gaining the spiritual and emotional tools I needed to make sense of everything at the time. I basically accepted that it wasn't meant to be at that moment; cheesy and clichéd, but that was truly how I felt. I often had moments of what-if, but my greater focus was on trying to provide as much support as I could for my wife, who grappled with it a lot more. We aren't big on talking about such, although we do have our ways of deciphering each other and working through stuff ... I hope.

A couple of years later, we had been married for long enough to seriously contemplate starting a family. We figured that since it wasn't hard the first time, it would be easy this time around too. You do what you do without protection and babies come tumbling out. Yet, it just wasn't happening, no matter how much we tried. Eventually, we decided to see a specialist.

There are experiences in life that you have to go through to truly understand. What we see on television can create a slightly warped impression of what things are, how they work, how they look. Taking the medical route to conception is not a humorous, feel-good romantic comedy. It is a tense journey that can break people and relationships. The starting premise is to determine what is *wrong* with you so it can be fixed. Beginning with the negative can bring about feelings of inadequacy, which can manifest in less than positive ways.

Our doctor was an elderly man. The first thing he did was to put Estelle on the fertility drug, Clomid. Mood swings, discomfort and the chances of having a multiple pregnancy were very real. An instant family of five is not an impossibility.

My semen also had to be checked for quality, mobility and things of that nature. I have never felt so dirty. I remember walking into the clinic, the nurse giving me a plastic container, leading me to a room with a mildly worn leather La-Z-Boy and a side table with a couple of uncomfortably worn magazines, and leaving me with the following words: 'Please wash your hands, put the sample in the plastic tube and bring it through.' The sample! Imagine!

I had to go through this experience twice. The second time, due to the dismal nature of inspirational material in 'the room', I brought along my laptop, having spent about an hour the night before compiling suitable material collected from the internet. This second time was one of those experiences that would have made a great sequence of scenes in one of those romantic comedy films that I can't stand. It was early on a Monday morning – for some reason, that was their preferred day of the week. And any man will tell you, that is not the way one would like to start their day, especially a Monday. It leaves you sleepy and sluggish for the rest of the day.

Anyway, I settled into the same room, moving the magazines to make space for my trusty laptop and placed the necessary sample in the plastic container. I left them to clean the sample, which involves running it through a centrifuge, and hurried to the South African Post Office head office in Tshwane, where I was working at the time. After about two hours in the office, I had to rush back to Joburg, pick up said sample in a sealed test tube – with clear instructions to keep it at body temperature (you guess where I put it) – and went to pick up Estelle to go to the hospital for the sample to be given a helping hand to get one of the million minions to team up with its potential partner to do the whole cell division thing.

The thing was done. We waited. And waited. And nothing. I have since discovered that this attempt for offspring can be fraught with trial and tribulation, with more and more people struggling to conceive. Those more knowledgeable than I can probably explain it in detail, with extensive research to back it up, but I think the pace at which we live our lives today has a significant impact. That and the junk we put into our bodies every day. Our food has become so processed that we now have a name for anything that just hung out on a farm somewhere – free range.

It didn't work. There are certain things that have no words and this was one of them. Growing increasingly frustrated doesn't help either as it starts to become this self-fulfilling cycle. You need to be relaxed and not stressed, but the longer you go, the more stressful it becomes.

We eventually decided to move to a different fertility doctor, fortunately getting onto the patient list of a Dr Antonio Rodrigues, who is one of South Africa's best. Walking into his office for the first time, we immediately felt at ease, especially since everything was 'we' not 'you'.

After the first consultation to check things like mobility and stickability (don't think this is a word, but you know what I mean), he said we needed to come in early the following morning. This meant waking up at 4.30 am, doing the deed – half asleep, not in the mood – and then heading through to the clinic. You got to see the doctor on a 'first-come basis' (yes, there is a cheesy, childish joke in there somewhere) so there we were, in a room of people, all waiting, unified by the fact that we all had to wake up at dawn's crack in the same way. This was a reminder that, at its simplest, sex is often about procreation and not enjoyment.

There is something profound about looking through a microscope at these little bacteria-looking dots swimming around frantically ... the film *Look Who's Talking* took on a whole new meaning ... I could literally hear the conversations. I must admit that I was a bit sad knowing what the little fellas didn't ... they were on a microscope slide. There was to be no multiplying in the near and distant future.

After this, we also had to visit a nutritionist to determine what we each should be eating to ensure that our chances were significantly increased. To be honest, when we correlated the cost of the groceries for our nutrition schedules with what we had available in our collective financial stores, we decided that the nutritional diet thing was not within our reach.

It is said by some that the way to keep intimate relations going in a relationship is by ensuring that there are regular moments, even going as far as scheduling moments. To those I suggest they try the 'conception' schedule, which involves basically having sex for the purpose of procreation, and timing ovulation days – between day twelve and fourteen. If you ever want to kill love and passion, try that. It is guaranteed to seriously dampen the exciting, fiery bits that often come with spontaneity. Perhaps you need to wake up extra early or stay up really late to do the deed because life doesn't stop just because you are trying to make babies. I always had this image of tired and groggy-eyed sperm – reflecting my state of consciousness at the time – half-heartedly swimming up fallopian tubes, with running commentary in a similar fashion to the opening sequence of *Look Who's Talking*. 'Go on ahead, guys, I'll catch up.' 'After you ... no, really, after you.' 'I'm going to catch my breath leaning over here, good luck, fellas.'

There was also a minor operation in the middle of this for the missus and further tests for me, all with little success – or, at least, not immediate success. There is a level of patience required that can be impossible to reach. So many what-ifs. In these moments, you discover the true nature of a relationship. We marry for love and friendship as well as to build a family. What happens when you aren't sure that family will actually happen? What if it is going to be just about the two of you?

These are hard questions that start creeping in when going through this whole reality. It is a difficult experience that so few of us are prepared for as we have spent our adolescence and early adulthood constantly trying to ensure that there are no pregnancies. Then, when you want it, it doesn't want to come.

We realised that a lot of it had to do with our mental states, but how do you settle when the thing you want so badly just won't happen, no matter how much you try and what you try? It is also about how we live our lives, what we eat, the stresses and pressures that weigh heavily on us on a daily basis. All of this fuels and becomes a self-fulfilling prophecy that sucks you deeper and deeper into the abyss. The harder you try, the more faint a possibility it becomes. The doctor had done all he could for us. It was now simply a matter of trying and hoping.

We reached the point where we figured 'what will be, will be'. We got on with life, knowing that if we were destined to have children we would. Fortunately, we did. And, when we found out Estelle was pregnant with Kweku, she was already three months in. We were living life as fully as we could and Kweku came to add to that life. With Ayanna, we didn't think about it. We continued to live our lives and, four years after Kweku, she arrived, completing the family that we always wanted.

Permission granted

THE IDEA of a 'visa' from your wife to go out has always been strange to me. It feels like you are transferring from the rules of your home (and parents) to the rules of your wife, when, actually, you are building a life together, with 'together' being the operative word. One shouldn't need permission from their partner.

On my wedding day, I was asked if I was nervous, which I found a peculiar question. If I didn't want to get married, all I had to do was keep my mouth shut and not propose. I had started the ball rolling; on a random evening, while chilling and watching videos, I looked over and said, 'This is nice, let's get hitched.' I was under no pressure to do so. Yes, Estelle was pregnant at the time, but we had already established that we could have and raise a child together without being married, as long we were both committed to doing that, which we were.

After getting married, Estelle was the one who expressed concern that 'we didn't go dancing any more'. I was all danced out and, on that day, the precedent was set. She wants to go out, she goes out. I want to stay home, I stay home. We did have an incident though, about four years into our marriage, when I went out with a cousin of mine and she called at 4 am to find out where I was. I was dumbfounded. I pointed out that, for four years, she had gone out till the early hours of the morning without my hounding her.

I do expect her to update me, but that comes from concerns for her safety as opposed to monitoring her. I always say she should phone me, regardless of time, when she is leaving a place to come home. Instead she sends a text, which I don't hear. This is a point of contention, but we'll get there.

If I was inclined to run the streets, it would have to take her into consideration, which is what any relationship should be about: understanding and trusting your partner enough for them to live their lives, which, while it includes you, is not just about you, and vice versa.

Estelle and I are opposites in our temperament, our personalities and even in many of our interests. Not long after we got married, we were interviewed for a women's magazine. The theme was Unlikely Couples. Estelle was a programme director at a business school, and I was trying to make some type of living primarily through poetry. In their mind, the interview was to figure out how a corporate, professional career woman managed to be in a relationship with a tattooed, earring-wearing, afro-having artist.

What they got, instead, was an extroverted, outgoing, relatively carefree woman who enjoys hosting and socialising married to an introverted, serious, sometimes grumpy, strict man who can be inflexible with his approach to the world and life. What they were looking for was assumptions based on stereotypes.

I've always viewed relationships as twofold. Firstly, you have two unique individuals coming together to build a life. What worked for others, and the tips one used to find in women's magazines, won't necessarily work for everyone. Secondly, I have never bought into this idea of 'two becoming one' because I believe that, when two become one, one ends up swallowed.

I view any type of life partnership like the Olympic rings or the rings in the Audi logo. It is two rings, two people, finding enough overlap to justify the attempt to build a life together. The two individuals remain two distinct individuals and that is what they bring to the relationship.

I see the overlap as being about values because values guide how we live, the decisions we make, the actions we take. It comes with compromise and sacrifice, not in a negative sense, but rather with the reality that you can't build a life with someone when you aren't willing to budge on the things that you want to do. The values are the boundaries, the non-negotiables, but everything else should be evaluated and re-evaluated on the basis of the collective.

I read somewhere that to expect one individual to be everything to you is asking for the impossible. Trying to force this will leave you in a place where you need permission and that is not conducive to a sustainable relationship.

A partnership

She speaks
And I listen
Without judgement
With expectation
Without preconception

Her life is hers to live
As is mine
Together we shall conquer the world
The destination is the same
But, sometimes
Only sometimes
The paths we take
Are not the same

BEING IN THE WORLD

Scratch beneath the surface

A SYMPTOM of this age of information, with the internet, social media and devices constantly in our hands, is that there is so much noise, which can become overwhelming. These platforms have given us voice and enable our voices to carry beyond our immediate circles. It has created a situation where we cannot, and should not, take anything at face value.

You have to scratch beneath the surface. You have to look at what isn't being said because, often, that says more than what is being said. You have to be discerning. You have to go beyond what is being said and look at who is doing the saying. You have to be able to tap into the nuances.

Someone I admired when I was growing up was Malcolm X and he once said in a speech, and I am paraphrasing, 'Don't believe everything I say just because I am Malcolm X. Listen, absorb, process and decide whether it makes sense to you.'

This is a principle I have tried to apply to life, in general. Working in the media, I learned how we can use images and words to direct and misdirect attention. Seeing the image of a person always frowning or looking aggressive has an impact on your perception of that person.

Being repeatedly told in different ways that a person is this or that type of person also has an impact on how we perceive them over time. We see that so much in the African context. Most Africans have stories of travelling somewhere and being asked whether we live with wild animals, or if we have phones, traffic lights and cars or how did we learn English? We are all flawed, but there are those whose flaws are held up as the whole. Africa is not all war, disease and famine.

Kwame Nkrumah, Patrice Lumumba, Winnie Madikizela-Mandela, Steve Biko, Malcolm X, Thomas Sankara, Fidel Castro, Che Guevara, Sékou Touré, Bob Marley, Fela Kuti, Maya Angelou, Chris Hani ... the list is long. These are all people who I have drawn inspiration from – intellectual, spiritual and otherwise – while recognising that they are not perfect. I admire them for the good without being blinded by the not-so-good.

I find that in South Africa, perhaps because of history and the effectiveness and brutality of apartheid, there is a collective desire to put people on a pedestal. In a way, it is an attempt to find validation. It is not only South Africa but, having lived in the country for a significant portion of my life, it seems more pronounced. People take one positive and paint the whole human being with it. In a way, it is as if excelling in one thing automatically makes one a perfect human being.

The morning it came out that Oscar Pistorius had, allegedly, at the time, shot and killed his girlfriend Reeva Steenkamp, I had a radio interview where I was asked my opinion as to whether he did it intentionally or not. My response was that I did not know him personally so I did not know what type of person he was and, therefore, I would not speculate on it. That I left to those better qualified than I to make the judgement. As a former sprinter, I marvelled at his athletic ability and his journey through extreme obstacles to realise his athletic dreams, but that was the extent of my admiration.

I have an internal line that, when crossed, any admiration I may have for someone goes out the window. There is no logic to it, no list of criteria, I just know when it has been crossed. That is the compass I use, nothing more, nothing less.

I grew up on R. Kelly's music, from when he was just another voice in Public Announcement, like so many others did. I even forgave him when he took Aaron Hall's look and style – I was and am a huge Guy fan. When he supposedly married fifteen-year-old singer Aaliyah, I, with so many others, tried to pretend it was not a thing, plus it was not that clear whether it was the case at the time. When he went on trial for allegedly urinating on a young girl while sexually molesting her, I kind of believed that it was not him in the video, like he said.

Then, sometime around 2013, I read an interview in *Village Voice* with American music journalist Jim DeRogatis, who had spent years gathering evidence and reporting on R. Kelly sexually abusing minors. The interview and article were done by journalist Jessica Hopper, who was forthright about how she did not believe DeRogatis for years. On that day, the line was crossed, and I stopped playing or listening to his music. I made no announcement or proclamation and would only mention it to friends if it came up in conversation. Estelle, of course, knew because at home I did state that we do not listen to R. Kelly.

And then, in 2019, the docu-series *Surviving R. Kelly*, produced by filmmaker and writer dream hampton, was released and the world finally took note. Radio stations across the globe took his music off their playlists. At the same time, the discussion about separation of the man from the art started to gain traction. Don't get me wrong. The man is a musical genius and some of his songs have been significant in my life's soundtrack. For a long time, long beyond their lifespan on the music charts, the albums *12 Play* and *Chocolate Factory* were on high rotation at home.

I cannot reconcile that with what he is said to have done and, in this instance, I would prefer to sacrifice any type of enjoyment and write him off. It is a personal decision. I sleep better at night having made that decision. It is not a judgement of others. We are each responsible for ourselves and do things, hopefully, that we are at peace with.

A friend posted on Facebook one day that he was going to celebrate R. Kelly's music over ten days because he was comfortable separating the man from the music. I unfriended him for two weeks after telling him I would, and then sent him a friend request afterwards. Some may see this as a tad extreme, but I try to live by that inner compass, for me, not for anyone else.

In a way, it is this approach that drew me to hip hop and how it has been a part of my life since my early teens. Although I grew up in the only country in the world landlocked by a single country, although I grew up in a country where television programming came from the country we were surrounded by, our influences went much further than that. We did not depend on South Africa and the powers that be to mould what we listened to, what we consumed and what we were able to enjoy.

Being in a school, and a society, that had multiple nationalities, and having friends whose parents became diplomats or travelled around the world to live, work and study, there were other ways of accessing music and pop culture. I had a cousin who used to send video tapes of multiple episodes of the classic television show Yo! MTV Raps. We grew up listening to everything from Britpop to house and R&B to rock. It was about what resonated as opposed to genre.

Visiting Germany represented a continuation as opposed to an introduction to new music. I was listening to Guy, Al B. Sure, MC Hammer, Maxi Priest, Bell Biv DeVoe, AC/DC, Public Enemy, Jungle Brothers, Color Me Badd, Anita Baker, Soul II Soul, Seal, Massive Attack and everything in-between.

When I went to university in Durban in 1992, I still remember a friend bursting into my room to tell me about this new music form called rap and wanting to school me in it because he had heard Dr Dre's *The Chronic* for the first time.

What I connected with, beyond the enjoyment factor, when it came to hip hop was how it felt like a community with a philosophy as opposed to simply a music genre. The four elements of hip hop are deejaying, emcing, graffiti and breaking (breakdance). The fifth element is knowledge of self. This is said to come from the influence and teachings of the Nation of the Gods and Earths (the Five Percenters), an offshoot of the Nation of Islam, founded by Wallace Fard Muhammad in 1930 and led by Elijah Muhammad at its peak in the 1950s and 1960s. The Five-Percent Nation was established in 1964 by Allah the Father (Clarence 13X) after he left the Nation of Islam.

The Nation of Islam has what are called Lost-Found Lessons, which detail the ideology and philosophy of the religion. Allah took specific lessons and built the Five Percenter philosophy from those, in particular, Lost-Found Lesson No. 2, questions 14 to 16:

- 14. Who is the 85%? Answer: The uncivilised people; poison animal eaters; slaves from mental death and power, people who do not know the Living God or their origin in this world, and they worship that they know not what – who are easily led in the wrong direction, but hard to lead into the right direction.
- 15. Who is the 10%? Answer: The rich; the slave-makers of the poor; who teach the poor lies – to believe that the Almighty, True and Living God is a spook and cannot be seen by the physical eye. Otherwise known as: The Blood-Suckers of the Poor.
- 16. Who is the 5% in the Poor Part of the Earth? Answer: They are the poor, righteous Teachers, who do not believe in the teachings of the 10%, and are all-wise; and know who the Living God is; and Teach that the Living God is the Son of man, the supreme being, the (Black man) of Asia; and Teach Freedom, Justice and Equality to all the human family of the planet Earth. Otherwise known as: Civilised People.

While I am somewhat ambivalent to these categorisations, the idea of understanding oneself, understanding the power and voice that you have, by working on the self, is what most resonated with me and I have tried to live my life accordingly.

Key concepts in Five Percenter teaching and thinking include Supreme Mathematics and Supreme Alphabet, where different numbers relate to different concepts, namely:

1. Knowledge
2. Wisdom
3. Understanding
4. Culture or Freedom
5. Power or Refinement
6. Equality
7. God
8. Build or Destroy
9. Born (Birth)
0. Cipher

I never went deep enough to understand how it works, but my layman's interpretation of the importance of each of the above when navigating life has always been a given. It means being committed to constantly evolving, constantly growing, constantly becoming a better version of myself as part of a community, a society and a species.

I try to teach my children to scratch beneath the surface, encouraging them to engage more with the world beyond just the exterior. Hopefully they will understand that who we associate with, who we hold up and who we admire all rub off on us, whether we like it or not, and start to develop an inner compass or intuition that allows them to make decisions that they are comfortable with.

Be you

I WAS taught to accept myself for who I am. I was taught that the easiest thing to be is yourself, because the energy that would be spent crafting and maintaining a particular image or persona can be better spent on discovering yourself. Living is the process of finding who YOU are.

I wasn't always so comfortable with this idea. Being a little shy and introverted, the world around me often said that there was something wrong with me. Being constantly told that you are 'antisocial' because you prefer your own company eventually takes up residence in your mind. The world is built for extroverts.

It took me some years of living, and maturing, to recognise that there is nothing wrong with me just because I would prefer not to be around crowds, or I am not good at starting up conversations and making small talk, or I still struggle with cold-calling, or walking into spaces where I don't know anyone.

In high school, I had a girlfriend who would often kick me under the table when I was talking to people because it seemed I was being offensive or rude, even though, in my mind, I wasn't. I came to the realisation that, sometimes, the way I put words together and my tone can be interpreted negatively, even when that is not my intention.

This is probably why I have a small circle of friends who all understand how I communicate and why I do some of the things I do, and don't take offence when it isn't intended. I sometimes find new people tedious because you have to go through the whole process of understanding each other.

I am by no means perfect. In the areas where I feel I need to be and do better or change, I work on them. The key here is 'I'. It isn't about what others may feel I need to change about myself but what I feel I need to change.

Hater has become part of the lexicon. When someone doesn't like you, they are labelled a hater. In the early days of Twitter, I used to jokingly call myself President of the Hateration Nation because each of us could be labelled hater in different situations. Plus, the simple reality is that not everyone will like you. Not everyone will find you interesting, amazing, fascinating, entertaining, funny, intelligent, creative and generous. Often, there is no logic to it. There doesn't need to be. It is called being human. And so, if you don't like me, that doesn't make you a hater, it just makes you someone who doesn't like me.

If someone doesn't like you, that should not be your problem. It shouldn't be something that consumes your time and your energy because, most often, you are not going to be able to change their mind. Spend the time on those who do like you, as well as yourself.

The pie isn't one size

I CAN be as competitive as the next person, or, at least, I used to be when I was younger. I played multiple sports, excelled as a 100-metre sprinter, and so I could not help but be competitive. Plus, in modern society, the individual is defined as the ultimate unit, even when it flies in the face of how, for Africans in particular, the collective is more important.

Scarcity has reinforced this with the divide between the haves and the have-nots increasing exponentially, regardless of how much we cry about it. Plus, it feels more like lip service than genuine concern. Instead, we become even more competitive, to the point of brutality. Look around the world. Look at the history of the African continent. It is a given that, from a resource perspective, we are the richest continent on the planet and yet, as a result of the constant scramble for our resources that started with colonialism and continues with the West and China, we are often seen as the poorest. There are many who see us as merely being here to exploit.

We take advantage of each other without thought because we see scarcity and limitations everywhere. In business, our competitors are to be crushed and/or put out of business. Corruption is the order of the day because we feel the need to amass as much as possible, usually at the expense of others. Although it may sound utopian, there is a place for all of us.

Look at the amount of food that is thrown away the world over instead of being given to those who need it. A friend of mine, who was a waiter in the US while in high school, once told me how his manager reprimanded him when he wanted to take leftover food for the homeless people in his area. The reasoning was that if something happened, the restaurant would get sued.

We waste terribly and then bemoan the scarcity that exists in the world. We have bought into the narrative that the pie is available in one size and, therefore, if you have an appetite for a bigger slice, it can only come at the expense of others eating from the same pie.

Allow me to wander off a bit and talk about love-songs. I am a sucker for a great love song. If you were able to count and document every single love song ever written, you would probably come up with millions. And yet, every day, more and more love songs are being written and recorded. How is that possible? I consider Donny Hathaway's cover of Leon Russell's 'A Song for You' as close to perfect as you could get in a love-song performance. Yet, there have been other songs since written and recorded, which, in my opinion, are as perfect. We can only listen to a certain number of songs over a lifetime; yet, more and more songs continue to be created and, for most of them, there is an audience.

How many things have been invented since the dawn of humankind? We still look at the pyramids in awe and wonder, still try to figure out who built them and how they were built in a time when the machinery and technology that we have today were non-existent. There are those who believe that aliens built them. And maybe they did. Every era brings with it wonders that those who lived just before could not imagine. I used to look at my father and his generation with awe. They were navigating cars, smartphones, televisions and video machines, having been born in a time and place where a bicycle was a luxury and, at most, you were able to access the radio. All of these things materialised during their lifetime and have a place.

I remember when cellphones came on the market. I remember when televisions did not have remotes. I remember when my father's secretary used a typewriter and I remember the wonder of an electronic typewriter. I remember having to listen to World Cup matches on the radio. I remember the time before social media. I remember the first Betamax video machine before the VHS tape, DVDs, Blu-ray and streaming services. I remember being in Germany and only being able to phone my family in Lesotho about four times – birthdays and Christmas – because it was so expensive to call. The cheaper option was writing letters, which could take weeks to arrive and it would take a few more weeks for the response. I remember my father sending postcards from his travels and often only receiving them when he returned. I remember how amazing it was to get a Walkman and how I could listen to my music on cassette while in motion. Hell, I even remember spending money on a cassette player for my car that could play both sides without you having to take it out and turn it around.

Yet, we continue to invent and there continues to be a place for new creations and inventions. While some things fall by the wayside, other things pick up the slack and carry us forward. Yes, sometimes, for construction to happen, destruction needs to take place first. And, on occasions, people make the wrong decisions, and we end up with the end of Kodak or Nokia or similar, but, in aggregate, there is addition to the collective as opposed to subtraction.

All of this is to simply say that there isn't just one pie, so we do not have to be at each other's throats, grabbing for a bigger piece of the pie. We can make more pie, with everyone getting their own pie. In fact, some of us may not want pie and lean towards pizza or pastries. This is my lesson as I have grown older, matured (hopefully) and become less competitive. There is a space for each of us. It is about perspective. And the collective. Without losing sight of the individual but also without making the individual the be-all-and-end-all.

The hermit

AT A Mind Power seminar that I attended in 2018 run by John Kehoe, he said, 'You are not your mind,' and it blew my mind. I am still trying to get a handle on it, but it opened up thoughts I had never really considered up to that point. I have lived firmly in my head most of my life. The voice that keeps going non-stop in my head is, was, me, in my entirety. We have spent a lifetime together, this voice and I. We have battled the world together, even when others were not in our corner.

I mean, I did teenage angst really well. There was a shadow that hung over me constantly. With hindsight, I lived with an underlying sadness that, perhaps, could be considered depression. As a teenager, I could go through joy, anger, excitement and sadness in the span of ten minutes. I was moody in the truest sense of the word. I would withdraw completely when things weren't going my way. Looking back, I wonder how and why my friends and family put up with me.

Everything about my life reinforced the idea that 'I am my mind'. With my older sister Grace eleven years my senior and my brother Kweku five years younger, there was no one going through the life stages with me. At home, I spent a lot of time alone.

As a Rotary Exchange Student, you stayed with a family for four months before moving on to the next one. It was your responsibility to adapt to them and their lifestyle and not the other way round. There were many moments when I would withdraw for my sanity, even with the wonderful families I had.

First in Germany and then when I moved to Joburg, I would often go out alone. In Germany, I would take the 30-minute train ride from Oldenburg to Bremen, just to go clubbing at a nightclub frequented by the American GIs stationed at a base close by. It was the only club where I would get to listen to hip hop and R&B, which is why I went. Occasionally, I would make a friend or two, hang out for the night, never to see them again; other times, I would party on my own.

In Joburg, I would jump into my car on a Sunday night and just drive, eventually ending up in the Sandton City shopping mall, window-shopping at 11 pm. I also occasionally went clubbing on my own. There was 206 in Orange Grove, which was the one place they played hip hop, drum & bass and jungle. I came across it on the way home from a friend's place and walked in because I saw cars outside and I was curious. For a short while, I used to go there alone, talking to no one but the bartender. I did eventually run poetry sessions there and made friends I would bump into there.

Being a bit of a hermit has its benefits but can become burdensome when you have a family. In my first year of marriage, as we were trying to find our rhythm, my tendency to get home and not want to talk created some tension in the house. There were days when I got home, said hi and then sat playing the game Age of Empires through the night. Estelle would repeatedly ask me what was wrong and struggled to make sense of there being absolutely nothing wrong; I just didn't feel like talking.

When Kweku was born, it became harder to reconcile my need for alone time with the growing family. In the periods when I worked from home, I would literally sit in my office for hours on end, well into the early hours of the morning, writing, plotting, tweeting. When Kweku started at kindergarten, I would wake up to get him there by 8 am and then sit back in my office, often for the rest of the day, into the night. I would come out to have supper with the family and then head back in.

I have become a lot more conscious of how easy it is to slip and get bogged down in my head. And, in learning that I am not my mind, it is slightly easier to pull myself back by recognising there is more to me, which includes my body and spirit. Plus, the mind is not singular; there is the conscious and the subconscious mind, each one needing to be acknowledged and fed.

Look, I won't lie. I still have hermit tendencies, but those moments alone are more constructive these days. I am a lot more mindful and a lot more present in the present. It is about wallowing less and experiencing more, even if it is in the mind. And it is about being able to step out and into the world.

Success + legacy = a life well lived

A BIG reason for my sudden decision to leave Maseru and the family businesses to move to Johannesburg was the political unrest in Lesotho in 1998. At the end of that year, a Southern African Development Community force, comprising the South African National Defence Force (SANDF) and the Botswana Defence Force, was asked to bring calm to Maseru's streets. When the SANDF armoured vehicles rolled into Maseru, there was widespread looting, and our offices, which were on the first floor of a building that also housed a KFC, ended up being partially burned. The chimney for the KFC ran through our reception and so, when that was set alight, the fire spread into our offices.

Baffoe & Associates had been in those offices for over fifteen years. We had to break down the door and salvage a lifetime of reports, documents, books and family papers – the burning smell on these documents lingered for years afterwards, no matter how much we aired them.

In the year before this, my father had been doing work for the CSIR in South Africa and I tried to convince him to move to South Africa, but he was settled in Lesotho. It was the country that he had made his home, and he wasn't going to leave to start again. At the time, there were also projects that I had been cultivating for some years, including the contract to produce Lesotho drivers' licences. I had it all worked out. I was going to be a millionaire by 28 in the year 2000. The management consulting and the selling of hair products and software solutions were going to pay off in a big way, and then the unrest, curfews and looting happened, setting the country and the family businesses back some years.

Young, frustrated and completely disillusioned, I needed a change of scenery. If my father wasn't going to make the move, I would. My younger brother, Kweku, was working in Joburg at the time so I moved in with him for a few months, deciding to gradually make the move to the city. Kweku then moved back to Maseru, while I stayed on to figure stuff out.

I worked out a deal with a family friend who has been like an older brother to me. He had a small furniture company, primarily producing corporate furniture but also some creative consumer furniture. In exchange for R150 an hour to help him improve the efficiency of the company, I had the space and time to travel back to Maseru every week and work out what it was I really wanted to do.

I eventually started BAKA Consulting, initially operating out of my brother's offices while my business partner operated out of where he was working at the time. We then rented offices in the same block. For the life of me, I can never understand the sometimes glamourised view of entrepreneurship and being your own boss. It is difficult for most of us. I had to move out of the townhouse I was living in because I couldn't afford rent. I moved in with Aunt Pam and I would often borrow R20 from her weekly for petrol to drive to my offices in Midrand, at least 15 kilometres away.

I left the business in 1999, which was followed by a flurry of jobs and projects, from working with a fashion designer to put on shows, being a booker at the agency Contractors, freelancing for an event company and working at a small record label to consulting at the South African Post Office, being a poet, lecturing at Damelin college and working for a television production company.

Money was erratic, even when I looked extremely accomplished from the outside. Meanwhile, those around me were making real money. I eventually reached the point where I was forced to redefine the idea of success and, by extension, legacy. For years, it was framed around material wealth, but, considering that has always been fleeting for me, I needed a different perspective, for my sanity, at least.

In a way, my journey has mirrored my father's. While he had moments of financial success, his success, in my view, was tied to what he had accomplished over his lifetime. When he passed away, I received a seemingly random phone call from a man in Botswana who wanted to offer his condolences. My father had been his lecturer in the early 1970s in Kampala. At the funeral, there was a group of at least three young women who were helping out. They were my father's other children in that he had put them all through school, and they weren't the only ones. And there was the young Mosotho man who sent me a direct message on Instagram three months after my father had transitioned. My father had forced him to sit down in his office to apply for a prestigious fellowship at a university in the US because he was procrastinating about it. He messaged me to thank me for what my father had done.

These are all measures of success and, to get to them, you need to live your life with that in mind, with the understanding that what you do doesn't just impact you but those around you. There are two parts to it, in my mind. Are you, and your family, able to live the lifestyle that you envisage and want for yourself? And do you leave your little patch of the world better for your having been in it? Money is merely a vehicle, a facilitator that makes the above easier to accomplish. I want to be able to spend my days writing, travelling, pursuing creative projects that fulfil me. I want to be available for my family, to share in experiences with them that enrich us all as human beings. Money makes this easier to do. It isn't the end goal.

In the words of Yasiin Bey (formerly Mos Def) from his song 'Umi Says': 'I ain't no perfect man / I'm trying to do / the best that I can / with what it is I have.'

When they look back over my life, I hope that they will be able to say, these words epitomise how I lived.

4 words

i travel backwards in search of a future that dreams are made of

i travel backwards over oceans and seas
and see ships laden with human cargo
bodies tortured and beaten
hearts wounded and bleeding
souls demeaned and weeping
all in the name of commerce

and i travel backwards in search of a future that dreams are made of

i travel backwards and see men dying for reasons unknown
war, disease and hate plague a world
that seeks humanity beyond the profanity
a world that continues to dream and believe beyond the insanity

and i travel backwards in search of a future that dreams are made of

i travel backwards over time itself
the clock spinning uncontrollably in reverse
through days and weeks and months and years and decades and centuries
blindly repeating history in its full glory
reducing life to its true folly

and i travel backwards in search of a future that dreams are made of
i travel backwards through galaxies in search of my grail
i orbit the sun and journey from mercury to pluto to beyond
i surf the milky way, flitting effortlessly between speckled stars
that reach out with light and mystery
my path is mirrored off satellites that spread a distorted human agenda
civilisation avoids my call for help and the earth's gravity pulls me back home

and i travel backwards in search of a future that dreams are made of

i travel backwards and see my ancestors
as kings and queens
warriors and priestesses
gods and goddesses
roots straddling culture and religion
tradition embedded in hearts with minds open to change
the old moulded and merged with the new
history planted, watered and blossoming into a brighter tomorrow

and i travel backwards in search of a future that dreams are made of
i travel backwards in search of a future that dreams are made of

i know it sounds like a distant illusion but, you see,

i am but a drop in a raging ocean bashing against the rocks to reach the shore
i am one of many voices that crawl through society's stench in search of truth
i am one of many hearts that seek the beauty in the mud piles of human history
i am one of many souls that believes in a universe that can only expand into greatness
and i travel backwards in search of a future that dreams are made of

i travel forwards and dream of a future built on my travels backwards
never halting, never faltering, never losing sight of my vision
because my dreams shall become a reality
and without dreams what else is there to believe in

and so, i travel backwards in search of a future that dreams are made of
i travel forwards and dream of a future built on my travels backwards
i travel forwards and dream of a future built on my travels backwards
i travel forwards to a future built on dreams
i travel forwards to a future
i travel forwards
i travel forwards
i travel
i travel
i

When death do us part

I HAVE a tattoo on my calf that incorporates the Grim Reaper, a sugar skull and wings coming around onto my shin, where there is an hourglass with the sand pouring out of the bottom into another skull. The design was inspired by a 100-word email to the tattoo artist, in which I attempted to explain my relationship – if you can call it that – with death.

Despite the deaths of my mother, grandmother and uncle at such an early age, I didn't experience the grief that comes with the death of anyone close to me again until I was in my teens, when a school friend was killed. My father always represented the family at funerals and I rarely went. Yet, in spite of this fortunate run, I was considered a tad morbid as a teenager, fascinated by skulls and the occult and the like. Plus, I never thought I would live past my mid-twenties. Now I hope to live for a very long time, but I am still drawn to skulls.

My gradual change of heart was probably influenced by what some have derogatively called 'New Age' religion, which I went through in my late twenties when I started exploring shamanism, and the world of spirits and ancestors. For most of my teens, I was what my English teacher described as a 'freethinker', someone who does not believe there is a God, without being presumptive enough to say there is no God, but rather tries to live their life to the best of their ability, in harmony with the world around them. As a side note, I discovered much later that this is an actual school of thought or movement – there was no Google in the 1980s.

The Freedom from Religion Foundation defines a freethinker as 'a person who forms opinions about religion on the basis of reason, independently of tradition, authority, or established belief. Freethinkers include atheists, agnostics and rationalists. No one can be a freethinker who demands conformity to a bible, creed, or messiah. To the freethinker, revelation and faith are invalid, and orthodoxy is no guarantee of truth.'

This is, frankly, a step further than I am comfortable with. My approach to religion, which is greatly influenced by the home I was raised in, has always been 'each to their own' as long as it helps them make sense of the world and does not impose on the lives of others. Atheism has invariably seemed like its own religion and I have never been comfortable with proclaiming 'there is no God'. My siblings, especially my older sister, are Christians, my wife is Christian (having been raised Catholic) and my children consider themselves Christian. And I have friends who are Muslim, Jewish, Buddhist and Hindu.

What I connected with was spirituality, outside of any type of organised religion. I'm not good at being told what to do and prefer to find my own way through it. It is a little ironic that, considering the perception of it, what actually opened me to spirituality were my interactions with the Church of Scientology, starting with the rehab process, called the Purification Rundown, which I went through at the end of 1999, and then several courses and sessions I completed between 2000 and 2001.

When I reached the point where I felt I had gained all I could gain from Scientology, I walked away.

The crazy thing is that twenty years later, I still get phone calls, messages and emails, all trying to get me to come back into the fold. I constantly have to repeat that, while I am grateful to Scientology for helping me navigate a difficult time in my life and opening me up to spirituality, there is no chance of my going back. It would feel too much like going backwards. Using what I learned there as a launchpad of sorts, I have explored African spirituality, shamanism, reiki, tarot and even the use of crystals, particularly for body alignment.

This has brought me closer to an understanding of what I believe happens when we die. Although still not fully clear, I do feel that the soul ventures out into the ether, somewhere, and there continues to be a connection of sorts with the physical realm. My ancestors watch over me and I feel their presence at times. Now, if you want to call that 'heaven', because it gives you comfort, cool.

This line of thought or feeling was inspired by two specific experiences. The first was during a body alignment experience. I was lying on a raised massage-type bed with my eyes closed while the practitioner – let's call her Jane – was aligning my chakras using crystals. She was coming to the end, holding a crystal over my head. Suddenly I felt a burning sensation in my left foot, which snaked its way up my leg slowly, over my ankle, shin, knee and thigh before going away as abruptly as it started.

After the session was over, Jane asked me if I had felt a sensation in my leg, to which I responded 'yes'. She described it, including exactly where I felt it. I had opened my eyes briefly, so I knew it wasn't her. The explanation she gave was that it was my mother, obviously in spirit form, who had stood over me, smiling as she gently ran her celestial hand up my leg.

For some reason, that was the first time I both realised and had to confront how angry I was at my mother for deserting me, irrational as it was. At 30 years old, for the first time, I was able to acknowledge this, which made it easier to then work through that anger. It was also the first time I started building a relationship with my mother, where she was more than just the woman in the photographs.

Whenever I think or talk about her, it usually means that she is present. I sometimes have conversations with her and say goodnight to her every night. I have now added my father, my friend Gerrard and my mother-in-law Elaine to the list. It may be a little out there for some, but it has helped me stay sane and, to a certain extent, navigate loss and grief.

The second experience was during my consultation with Lionel Berman, who uses what he calls 'clairaudient and clairvoyant powers to convey to you the messages and teachings of the Spirit Guides' with tarot cards. This was when Estelle had the miscarriage and he told me that our daughter was actually my mother's soul and her mission was to fast-track and solidify our relationship.

People may leave us physically, but they never leave us spiritually.

They may not always be with us, but they are often there for us. It also does not need to make sense to others, and I am not always able to articulate it, but I know it to be true, for me, in the same way that a believer of a particular religion finds comfort in certain views. Faith is not logical in the same way that love isn't.

When Elaine, who was living with us, passed away in 2013 Estelle and Kweku took it extremely hard. Ayanna was nearly two years old, so it was difficult for her to grasp what had happened. Kweku found comfort in the belief that she had gone to heaven. Estelle found comfort in her Christian faith and beliefs. In all honesty, I had no way of articulating something that still doesn't make perfect sense to me with a six-year-old who had just lost his granny.

Just as my father allowed us to find our own way, my approach is to expose my children to different religions, without comparison or competition or expectation. I reinforce the thinking that we are each on our own path to find what works best for us. Whatever path one decides to take, it is important to understand that there is no global 'best way' and that we should not impose ours on the next person. And that those who have died have simply transitioned to a different plane. What is that plane? I cannot define it, but there is a comfort in knowing that death does not completely do us part.

Thriving mentees

THERE HAVE been people to whom I have looked for advice, knowledge and guidance, professionally and personally. Sometimes I have even approached them for that mentorship directly. It is an interesting relationship and the biggest takeaway for me has been that they are there just to simply provide advice, based on the wisdom they have gathered in their lifetime. The onus remains on me to both determine what makes sense to me, taking into consideration my own position and views, and to do the actual work, if it resonates. In essence, they are laying out the tools and the understanding and my part is to pick up what works and go forth.

To be honest, I never thought beyond this until I started mentoring people. I must confess that it still feels a little weird when I am approached because I am still on my own journey, but, in line with my upbringing and the values I was raised with, I do try to contribute in whatever way I can. In the words of Otto von Bismarck, 'Only a fool learns from his own mistakes. The wise man learns from the mistakes of others.' While I learn from my own mistakes, most times, why waste them on me alone if it helps another person navigate their life. And I have few qualms in sharing my missteps.

The one thing I never thought about, until the first time it happened, was the uncomfortable feelings of jealousy that arose when a mentee started thriving, while I continued to battle through my own projects. At the same time, there is a sense of pride in seeing someone succeed and logic says one should simply be happy; emotions, however, can be illogical.

A by-product of hurting my leg at university, and having multiple operations that rendered me partially disabled at the time, was a love for the Tour de France. After writing my June exams, I went home for the month-long holiday, where I spent three weeks homebound, stuck in the house, while the rest of the family went about their business. I spent most of this time on the couch, watching daytime television. Limited to soapies – I've never been a fan – I ended up watching full stages of the Tour, which can run for up to five hours.

Two things struck me about the Tour. Firstly, it is a travelogue of France. As the race winds its way through the different regions and small towns and villages, the commentators share the history of each place. Secondly, cycling is a team sport, with each team riding for the team captain, the sprinter, the climber and, lastly, potential stage winners. But the team captain is the primary focus. To watch a man put everything on the road just to ensure that his teammate is in the best position to succeed is a great lesson in selflessness and teamwork.

It is a lesson that I find I have to constantly remind myself of. When you are part of a collective, in some ways a faceless member of a team, there will be occasion when you won't agree with every decision or action that is made, yet you have to stand behind it and do everything you can to ensure that whatever it is that has been decided actually transpires.

This is what I use to remind myself when the unhealthy feelings arise about seeing someone who I have advised succeed. This and the reality that the person made the best decisions for themselves and did the work, which is why they succeeded. I am on my own journey and, perhaps, part of that journey is being able to do my part in making something easier or in making something make sense for a fellow human being. Therefore, their success means that I have succeeded, in a way.

Ideas – a dime a dozen

THEY LANGUISH in the bottom of a box in my storeroom. Small, black, hardcover notebooks, full of ideas. Their digital siblings sit in Word documents in multiple folders in the cloud, never looked at, simply floating in the ether. I have never struggled for ideas, concepts for businesses, television shows, poems or books. And I have been religious about documenting them. Sometimes scraps, short sentences, little paragraphs, to serve as reminders; other times, fully fleshed-out documents.

For years, they hung over me like a dark shadow, taking up mental space, only to be discarded when I saw someone else do something similar. I would then sit and lament how, if I had actually done something with that idea, I would be so much further in life or better off. They were monuments to the words of American minister and author Norman Vincent Peale, 'If you put off everything till you're sure of it, you'll never get anything done.'

Yet, there's another side to this. I went to see a business/life coach for advice and guidance on how to pull myself away from the edge of the crater that is procrastination and he had me undertake what became a painful exercise. He likened me to the circus act of spinning multiple plates on sticks, going back and forth to ensure that the plates kept spinning. The exercise was to list all my ideas, projects and things that I was going to do, one day. I then had to get a pack of paper plates, write each concept on a paper plate and stick them on the wall. I eventually had 30. I then had to prioritise them, in order of which I was able to do and wanted to do. The ones that I knew, in my heart of hearts, that I would never do, I had to discard, either by throwing the paper plate away or by giving it to someone who would do it justice.

I eventually got it down to ten or so, which, I suspect, is still too much, but, hey, I live a 'tapas' life, with multiple small projects adding up to a career of sorts. I now have four areas of operation, divided into Writing, Speaking, Consulting/Collaborations and Zebra Culture (which is what I call my play company to house things like merchandising and 'passion projects' that I may want to pursue, primarily in the media and content space).

Minimalism is not just the act of clearing out what is unnecessary materially. It is also clearing mind space and creating order to ensure that you can devote energy and thinking to the things that are a priority for you.

I now have no qualms about not getting things done. The truth is that if I end up doing something about something, I was meant to. If I don't, I wasn't meant to, at least right now. If I wake up one day and feel driven to do it, then it is now meant to be, even if it wasn't previously because ideas are truly a dime a dozen and there has been many a moment when I have become subservient to an idea, just because it looks or sounds cool. This is counter-productive and not conducive to my peace of mind.

Flaws and all

A BY-PRODUCT of regular and honest reflections of one's self is to come face to face with one's imperfections and flaws, repeatedly. No one is perfect, except perhaps the narcissist, but it is decidedly disconcerting to be confronted by these imperfections constantly. Self-doubt becomes a consistent companion and the feelings of inadequacy eventually attach themselves to your personhood. Each mistake you make, each action or reaction becomes an indictment of you as a human being.

When I wrote off my father's car, a year after I had an accident with the same car, I wrote him a letter to say that perhaps he was better off without me around because I was a bad son and, therefore, a bad human being. The disappointment and anger as a result the two accidents was, in my view, an indication that his life would run smoother if he did not have to deal with me. Fortunately, he did not take me up on the offer, instead giving me a lesson in how my flaws did not condemn me completely. The disappointment was not in me but in the thing that I had done.

When I briefly lectured at Damelin School of Business on the Principles of Management in the mid-2000s, at least 70 per cent of the group failed my first test. I wanted to quit. From my perspective, if fewer had failed, it would have been on them, but, because the majority had failed, the problem was probably me. Estelle, who was working at Damelin at the time and had helped get me the gig, convinced me otherwise and, by the end of the module, everyone passed.

We often take more to heart than we should. It has taken me time and life experiences to reach the point where I understand that a mistake does not make you a bad person. A moment – depending on the severity of that moment – shouldn't define the entirety of your being. A failure does not make you a failure. It is something that I need to regularly reinforce because there will always be those moments of relapse.

Broken pieces

In the mirror
All I see is the reflection
Of a broken and flawed being

He smiles a dreamy smile
Attempts to hide the confusion
Just beneath the skin

There are times
When the regrets feel so much heavier
And the doubt drags at the psyche

Ask for help

LOOK, LIFE can truly feel like an obstacle course you need to complete in the fog. Beyond the poor visibility, over the years our sight diminishes, our legs don't power forward like they used to, our reflexes slow and our mind struggles to make the connections needed to make it from this point to the next. We tap into previous experience to keep moving, but, sometimes, the baggage we accumulate along the way weighs us down. There were moments when we went left when we should have gone right, or vice versa. Everyone should have someone to whom they can turn when they need to make sense of things. Someone to help us discard these unnecessary weights that slow us down. Someone to help us peek into the shadowy parts of our minds and bring light. Preferably someone who has the tools to guide us. A professional someone.

I had a girlfriend in high school who wanted to be a psychologist. She eventually went on to become one; before that, she was the person I often turned to, even though some of what I was dealing with was centred on her and our relationship. With hindsight, I can, without a shadow of a doubt, say that I needed a therapist. I still have no idea if there were therapists in Lesotho at that time. It was so far off my radar, it could have been in another galaxy. Plus, as a boy becoming a man, that wasn't something you did.

Another way that this short-sighted view of what a man does and doesn't do manifests in the physical. You go through pain because you are meant to be strong, making the situation worse because you didn't seek help in the beginning. While I recognise this, the idea that, as a man, you have to power through things and be stoic in the face of pain is one that is still deeply ingrained in me. One would think that after nearly having my lower leg amputated because of the 'no pain, no gain' maxim, I would be quicker to react when I have physical discomfort, but I don't always do that. And I have to constantly stop myself from pushing that misguided thinking onto Kweku.

After my mother-in-law passed away, Kweku went to see the psychologist at his school. She assisted him to deal with the loss and grief. Two years later, he went back for several sessions. He was struggling to articulate his moods and emotions and, when angry or upset, he would withdraw to his room. Ironically, I was exactly the same at that age. I do hope that, while I powered through that turmoil and survived, seeing someone has helped him navigate it with much less pain.

There have been other occasions when he has gone back for some sessions, but it is also important to not create the impression that something is wrong with him and let him understand that this is a support base that he can tap into to ensure that he doesn't end up like his father.

Every time we went in to chat to the psychologist for feedback on her sessions with Kweku, all I could think was 'I need therapy'. I recognise this and I am not averse to it. I have long gone beyond the idea of a man as this emotionless being who bottles everything up inside. Yet, I still do that a lot: keep a tight rein on myself and my emotions. In learning and accepting that we can't control the world around us, I shifted that control to myself, wiring all of me very tightly together.

My father always said you must be independent and self-sufficient. You can't depend on others so depend on yourself. I have internalised that to the point where, while I recognise the importance of it, it is extremely difficult to actually ask for help, even for small things, even from those closest to me. If someone offers, I have become better at accepting help, but to actually ask ...

It becomes tedious spending so much time and energy trying to keep everything together. It is like trying to hold hundreds of magnets together with the same poles lined up. There are times when all I want to do is let go. Those are times when I need that external voice to help me keep going. I do the work on myself daily, but sometimes it feels like it isn't enough. One day, I will be able to figure out what I am afraid of and learn to ask for help. Hopefully, that day is soon.

Day one

Each day, the sun rises
Sometimes behind the cover of dark,
Cement coloured clouds
Sometimes, bright,
On your face,
Warming you up
From the inside
Starting with your bones

Each day, the sun rises
Sometimes cloaked
Sometimes uncloaked
But it always rises
And each day
When the sun rises
It is the first day
Of the rest of your life

Crawling out of the past

WHILE THE past has and continues to have a strong influence on my life, I have always been firmly focused on the future, often at the expense of the present. There was a time when I had a five-year and ten-year plan, but no idea what tomorrow was going to look like. In high school, we would sit and talk about where we would be in the year 2000. My vision of it was clear, if I was still alive. I would be a millionaire, involved in the family businesses and, as a result of my comfortable financial status, I would take off that year to complete a Master's in Economics at Harvard Business School or London School of Economics as what was called a 'mature student' in those days.

There was no vision of life beyond that, other than having a family, but it was a given that it would be financial bliss. As the universe is wont to do, by the time the year 2000 hit, during which I marked my 28th year, I was so far from that objective that it was laughable. I was a Jabu-come-lately, living in Joburg. I had just walked away from my IT consulting company with no plan. And I spent New Year's Eve at home at my aunt's house fresh from the Purification programme, sipping juice, unclear about the future.

The question of the meaning of life is one that has tripped up many a person. Society says we must go to school and then work – whether for yourself or someone else. It says we should find a partner, have and raise children and, some day, in the distant future, when we have retired, go out and experience life, as if we haven't been experiencing a version of it all along. It is a treadmill. We spend more time keeping our legs moving to avoid falling painfully on our faces, rather than moving forwards.

I listened to Eckhart Tolle's *The Power of Now* in 2017, in the aftermath of an eye procedure that forced me to spend a week with my eyes closed. All of a sudden, the importance of being present and focused on the Now made sense. Too much of my time had been spent lamenting about what had happened and worried about what could possibly happen. It brought to the fore what I had started to understand when I read Tim Ferriss's The 4-Hour Workweek. Design your life today.

Chatting to a friend during the hard COVID-19 lockdown in South Africa in mid-2020, he reflected on how the pandemic had forced him to consider what he was doing it all for. He was grappling with the question of purpose, of why he spent hours working hard for his employer, accumulating various items along the way – the house, the car, etc. – without taking a step back to consider the quality of his life and how it could be different in a fulfilling way. Unmarried and childless, he didn't have that as a motivation, which drives many of us with children. He didn't have to contend with what school they go to, what they need to help them live life, what he needs to buy for them – none of that.

In that moment, despite the seemingly endless challenges, I realised how fortunate I was, having gone through that process myself when I left *Destiny Man* in 2014. I have a clear idea of the lifestyle I want for myself and for my family. Very little of that is outward, about material possessions or based on the perceptions of my community; it is about the things that bring me satisfaction, fulfilment and contentment. And I get to spend a lot of my time working to be able to do and enjoy those things regardless of my financial state. Even the decision to perhaps get a permanent job is based on the overall objective. It isn't all-consuming but, rather, a means to an end.

Comparison is a surefire way to depress you because, materially, there will always be someone better off. When you consider yourself on the bottom rung of the ladder, if on the ladder at all, comparison can be debilitating because even halfway up can seem unattainable.

While I try not to allow the past to overrun the present, and I am learning to stay focused on the present, I have also learned to draw inspiration and motivation from the past: to recognise my accomplishments but not to dwell on them; to appreciate every moment, every experience that has made me who I am today but also to remember that each is just another chapter in the book of my life.

While I do not get as caught up in the future as I used to, I have learned to allow that image of the future to serve as a lens for what I do in the Now. My decisions in the present are guided by that future. If a decision or act brings me closer to that lifestyle, I go for it. If it doesn't, then I won't. Of course, sometimes I need to do things to make today easier, even when it isn't part of the master plan, but I do so consciously and with clarity. And then I switch back to what is most important. As Tolle wrote, 'Realize deeply that the present moment is all you have. Make the Now the primary focus of your life.'

Live by subtraction

THE ANALECTS *of Confucius* is a book on the sayings and wisdom of the Chinese sage Confucius and his students. In it, he is quoted as having said, 'At 15 I set my heart on learning, at 30 I know where I stood, at 40 I have no more doubts, at 50 I knew the will of Heaven, at 60 my ears were attuned, and at 70 I followed my heart's desire without crossing the line.'

Confucius from the Heart by Yu Dan brilliantly breaks down Confucius's key philosophies and, in the section that covers the above quote, Dan writes about how, when we reach 40, we start to live by subtraction, which resonated with me. The basic concept is that, when we are young, we accumulate things, but, as we grow older, we start to subtract the things that do not serve a purpose or are not in line with our purpose.

We have these 'age milestones' that society has deemed worthy of celebrating, for various reasons. Sweet sixteen. Becoming an adult and getting a key at 21. They were relatively significant for me, but it was turning 30 that was the most profound.

Overnight, I became more accepting of me as a human being, warts and all. My priorities started to change. I became more focused on me and what I wanted out of this thing called life.

The period between 27 and 30 was tumultuous. I thought I knew what I wanted out of life. I had a plan that was set in my teens that I was working towards. I turned 27 and everything was thrown up in the air. I had lived long enough to have experienced enough curveballs to force me to question everything, which resulted in my twenties ending with a somewhat painful re-evaluation. Turning 30, I found a semblance of balance and a new and improved life plan, including a recognition of the parts of me that I felt needed work.

Little did I know that turning 40 was not going to necessarily throw my life into chaos once again but rather bring me relief. All of a sudden, I had zero f**ks to give and I became comfortable with brutally subtracting that which no longer served my interests. I went from, deep down inside, wanting to be liked, wanting to please and worrying what people think of me to not really caring.

The word 'hater' has entered our lexicon to the point where you can't criticise people or dislike things any more. If you don't like a musician's music, or a film, or don't agree with something someone has done or thinks, then you are a hater.

The English monk and poet John Lydgate is quoted as having said, 'You can please some of the people all of the time, you can please all of the people some of the time, but you can't please all of the people all of the time.' The quote is also attributed to Abraham Lincoln, but Lydgate lived in the fifteenth century, so I am going to work with him as the originator of the quote.

Focusing on pleasing people can be a slippery slope, which I learned the hard way when editing *Destiny Man* magazine, in particular when choosing who to put on the cover. Every time an issue came out, I knew that I would be bombarded with multiple opinions from readers, the positive shared as passionately as the negative.

The lesson was that I needed to focus on what I felt was best and stand by it. I have carried this into all aspects of my life and have come to live by the words of actor Anthony Hopkins, who said, 'My philosophy is: It's none of my business what people say of me and think of me. I am what I am and I do what I do. I expect nothing and accept everything. And it makes life so much easier.'

My responsibility is to myself, my family, my community, and humanity, in that order. I do what I think is best and, I believe, everything else falls into place. And the reason why I start with the self? It's the reason why, in a plane, they tell you, in case of emergency put on your oxygen mask first before putting on the oxygen mask of your child. If you aren't good, how can you expect to help others?

Royalty

There are so many
Descendants of kings and queens
I wonder
Whether there is a place
For those of us
Who come from a long line
Of fishermen and farmers

Birds of a feather

ALL PARENTS see their offspring as the most beautiful, most intelligent, nicest, bestest children who ever graced the world, or at least they should. I have wondered whether parents of serial killers and murderers actually saw the signs. When I had children, I discovered how hard it is. I will defend my children in the outside world to the point of, well, extreme as it is, death.

My father had a lot to say about my friendships, especially when I had messed up. In his mind, my errant behaviour was only because I was blindly following my friends. While, on the one hand, it was complimentary that he saw me as inherently good and dutiful, on the other hand, he implied that I wasn't able to make decisions, even bad ones, for myself and was easily swayed by my friends.

The irony was that, while there were instances when I was a follower, there were also instances when I was the ringleader. Plus, if you have ever been part of a clique, you will know that the potential (mini) mob mentality is prevalent. All it takes is one person to introduce the basics of a bad idea for everyone to get carried away in the moment. One minute it's 'you heard about the party in the neighbouring town' and, before you know it, there are eight people packed into someone's parent's car that has been borrowed, without permission, on the way to the aforementioned party.

My father always said your friends should elevate you and you should elevate them, ensuring that, together, you are each becoming better for being friends. I get that now, as I turn into him. But it is also important that I reinforce this with my children, without disempowering them by assuming that they can do no wrong and it is other people's children who will always be the bad influence.

When I got a married, a friend recommended that I create some distance between myself and my single friends and, when going out, spend more time with friends who are in the same matrimonial boat. His reasoning was simple. If you are out and about and receive a call from your wife to come home, your single friends are more inclined to protest and accuse you of not being 'man enough' because you are at your wife's beck and call. Sadly, in many quarters, the idea of a man is still outdated, shallow and toxic. Your married friends will hopefully be more understanding. When a friend says, 'I only have an hour because I have to get home,' I don't need the details because I understand the responsibilities of being a husband and father.

Although I wasn't as extreme with the above recommendation, I have always tried to surround myself with kindred spirits. While the discussions about the importance of exposing yourself to people with differing opinions and the avoidance of echo chambers continue to rage online, I am particular about who I allow into my space.

Like my father, I know a lot of people, I have a lot of acquaintances, but I have few friends. Perhaps being an immigrant twice over and coming from a small family has something to do with it. I do think we use the word 'friend' flippantly and there is a blurred line between, for example, friend and close friend. I couldn't explain it but know it. In a way, there are those friends who become family and those who remain friends.

Estelle and I were meeting with our insurance broker to go over our portfolio. We were chatting about wills and he asked us a question that we had never considered. Who would raise our children if something happened to both of us? We had worked with the assumption that, if something happens to the one, the other will be there to raise the children. Sadly, life doesn't always work like that. My parents had worked on the premise that, because my father was nine years older than my mother, he would probably pass away first and, as a result, they planned off that basis.

Thinking about who will raise your children is intense because it isn't simply a material thing. If you are able, you probably have a life policy in place to ensure that those you leave behind will be covered financially. Raising children is not just about the things you provide your children but the values you seek to teach them. If you are no longer around, which of your friends do you feel will both love your children and instil the same values you would? It is also a huge responsibility you are asking someone to take on. Suddenly, the word 'friend' takes on a whole different meaning.

At the time, I had Gerrard. It was one of the easiest conversations I ever had, but then he passed away. I have been at a true loss ever since, exacerbated by how much harder it seems to be to establish strong, close friendships, the older I become. I must add, as a disclaimer, that I do have close friends, but another by-product of growing older is an increase in responsibility, so even the time spent together seems to diminish gradually.

Estelle has a close-knit group of friends, some relatively new, many spanning decades. Somehow, the bond between her and her friends seems to have grown stronger as they have gone through life stages. There was a time when we were part of a collective of families that did everything together. Christmas lunch and New Year's Eve parties. Spring picnics and days at the park. Birthday parties – for kids and adults – and afternoon braais, just for the sake of it.

Over the years, some of the couples have split up and I don't interact with the men much, showing how it was mainly the women who kept things together. Now, when there are gatherings, they are often smaller, with a bunch of children and their mothers. When I am not off doing my own thing, I frequently find myself the only man in a group of women.

I have long suspected that I am part of the problem when it comes to socialising. In the late 2000s, an editor from a South African newspaper I would occasionally write for gave me a men's recipe book called *Bloke* to review. In her mind, when I had 'the guys' over for a braai or to watch football, I could try out some of the recipes. It didn't make sense to her that I don't have people over, unless Estelle invites them, and I prefer to watch football, of which I am an avid follower, alone. When watching with others, there is too much commentary and analysis from the room. I am happy with both my own space and mumbling at the television solo. Hell, even though he and I supported the same teams – Bayern München, Liverpool and Kaizer Chiefs – I didn't enjoy watching with my father. I preferred to celebrate the results, when there was occasion to, with him, often over the phone.

I have gone from being in close proximity to my friends, many of whom I became friends with during my teens and my twenties, to being at a distance that doesn't diminish the bond, at least from my perspective. The foundation of these friendships is knowing that, when either of us is in need or is going through a special milestone, we will be there to support, even when we have gone months or years without actually seeing each other.

Hold your tongue

MY FATHER was opinionated. I am too. Yet, he was never vocal, outside of people close to him, about, for example, which political party he supported. He always said that when you are vocal about where you stand, especially on things like politics and religion, you create division because too many people still operate from a 'them-versus-us' perspective. We can have so much in common, but, because we support different political parties, we consider ourselves adversaries.

Sometimes I question whether I internalised that lesson to the extreme. I wonder whether I am doing myself and the world around me a disservice by being a silent supporter or dissenter, instead of standing at the front screaming and shouting.

I am more inclined to send whatever financial support I can to causes that are important to me than I am to stand and 'chant down Babylon'. I am the first to say we need to focus on doing the work as opposed to being seen to do the work, yet, sometimes, I am nagged by the feeling that I should be seen more.

A lot of what happens in society regarding violence against women, racism, misogyny, oppression and genocide feels performative. With social media, people are quick to speak out, change the avatars or profile pictures, and amplify hashtags, then move onto the next issue, as quickly. Or we sit and focus on what are the wrong things, in my view, wasting energy on discussing whether all #MenAreTrash, for example, when the work to be done is on how to stop the scourge of violence against women.

I try not to be as fickle. I try to do something regularly. I try to keep things top of mind. I also question whether I am doing things or going about things the right way, taking into consideration the reality that, even if I have the desire to help in particular ways, I may not always be in a space – mental, spiritually or otherwise – to help.

Guilt is such a destructive and unproductive emotion, but it creeps in occasionally. I try to remind myself that the measure of my contribution is over a lifetime as opposed to in a specific moment. I try to remember that it is important to use the questions, the uncertainty, as motivation to constantly reflect on and come back to contributing to causes that are important to me.

It doesn't have to be in the big gestures. My father put at least five young girls through various stages of school, and he influenced the lives of countless other people in different ways, helping them realise elements of their dreams. The world's problems can seem so overwhelming when you are looking to help. And 'compassion fatigue' is a real thing. As a result, I also remind myself of the importance of picking my battles, of focusing on the causes that I consider imperative and that I can tangibly contribute to in whatever way possible.

I may hold my tongue. I may worry that I am doing myself or others a disservice by doing so, but I console myself with the fact that my heart is in a good place and I will do the best that I can. While there will always be doubt, I do sleep with a relatively clear conscience.

All in due course

I RIDE a motorcycle. I had tried to ride one in my teens at a friend's house. I was able to move relatively steadily for about 10 metres, at which point, while attempting to do a U-turn, I somehow managed to drop the bike on my leg. Once they had stopped laughing, my two friends helped me out from under the motorcycle. I did not attempt to ride again for another twenty-odd years. It was probably for the best; I had moments of random recklessness when it came to driving. I went through a three-year period when I had a major accident each year.

And I used to drive fast, having learned how to drive on the open road on trips to the Eastern Cape, Johannesburg and Durban. My father had a rule. It should take X amount of time to drive to our destination. If we were delayed for whatever reason, like a detour, it was up to me to make up the lost time. When I moved back home after university for about two years, I would drive 200 kilometres to the town of Kroonstad every Friday, crossing the border at 4 am to be there in time to deliver the family's weekly newspaper to the printers. Sometimes, I would do another 200 kilometres to Johannesburg for a meeting or two, head back to Kroonstad to pick up the printed newspapers, drive home and deliver to the small depots that sold the newspapers.

On a good weekend, once I knocked off from work at 4.30 pm, I would head to Durban or East London or Mahikeng or Johannesburg for a weekend of partying, arriving back in Maseru in time for work on Monday. When I first moved to Joburg, I spent my weekends in Maseru for at least my first year. Sometimes, I would drive to Maseru on a Thursday night, spend Friday in the office, hit the streets that night, drive to Bloemfontein, about 160 kilometres away, on Saturday, party there and then drive up to Joburg on Sunday.

The reality is if I had a motorcycle at any stage during those years, I probably would not be sitting at my desk right now as a 40-something-year-old typing these words.

In my mid- to late thirties, the idea of getting a motorcycle became appealing. Some have called it a midlife crisis, but I do not believe in that concept. There was no crisis, and it was not destructive. And, when I decided that I was going to get a motorcycle, I went about it in what I consider 'the right way'. I enrolled in a novice course at the BMW Rider Academy, did a similar two-day course at the Harley-Davidson Riding Academy and have since completed another five courses, to ensure that I am as safe as one can be on a motorcycle.

I have had multiple lessons in things happening in due course, in doing things when the time is right, as opposed to when I wanted to. This could have been as trivial as when to read a particular book or as significant as when my children were born. There have been countless times when I have wanted to read a particular book, yet things seemed to get in the way of my settling down to it. When I do eventually read it, I realise that all those other times I hadn't reached the point, mentally, emotionally or intellectually, to grasp the contents. I, therefore, eventually read it when it would have the most impact on my life.

I wanted children when I was younger. However, I realised that because Kweku was born when I was 35, I had gone through enough growth to be calmer, more settled and mature enough to deal with fatherhood. The journey we took in trying to conceive put me in a better space to be a father.

Things happen when they are supposed to happen, regardless of how much we may think we want something. I don't see life as predestined but do feel that the lessons come when we are best placed to grasp them, for better or for worse.

South Africa is an angry country

WHEN THE wound is still so fresh that removing the scabs will draw blood, it is often hard to see beyond the pain. And when you are surrounded by the wounded, it is easy to internalise their pain. In 2018, I was working at the Gauteng-based radio station, Kaya FM, and we went on a content trip to Dakar, Senegal, which meant that we broadcast our shows from there. We also spent time visiting various sights in Dakar, including the UNESCO World Heritage Site of the Island of Gorée, which is tied to the dark history of slavery.

Gorée is a jarring place because, while the House of Slaves is still intact and there is a museum and memorial to the Atlantic slave trade, it is also home to Maison d'Education Mariama Ba, founded in the 1970s by Senegal's first president, Léopold Senghor, as a boarding school for girls who have achieved outstanding results in their national secondary-school exams. Mariama Ba was a Senegalese author and feminist, who is considered a pioneer of Senegalese literature. And on the early-morning ferry heading to Gorée, we were surrounded by people going to work, as we all do.

With our guide, a tall, distinguished and well-travelled Senegalese man called Hassan, we paid a visit to the House of Slaves and had the opportunity to sit down with the head curator. Having visited Elmina Castle in Ghana, I was probably better prepared for the visit than my colleagues, who were all South African. I was struck by the contrast in reactions. From my colleagues, it was immediate anger, bordering on rage; from Hassan and the head curator, it was a more balanced view of the place that dark history has in a contemporary world, which my colleagues, to a certain extent, struggled to understand.

Later on, I interviewed a Senegalese activist who spoke of work he was doing with a French corporation. When I asked him how he could work with the French, considering the colonial history, his response was that his approach was to ensure that whatever he did was on his terms. What I took away from that, and the Gorée visit, was that, while we need to take history into consideration, we can't let it cloud our minds. To ensure that it never happens again, we need to be deliberate in what we do today.

It is very much the perspective that my father raised me with. Having lived in Europe and Africa, having travelled extensively, interacting with people from diverse cultures and backgrounds, and, at the same time, being very cognisant of colonial history and how it continues to negatively impact our lives today, his approach, in essence, was to right the wrongs by consciously and deliberately ensuring that whatever he did today would create a different tomorrow.

The wounds in South Africa are still very fresh. In some ways, healing is yet to happen because we spent the first twenty years trying to gloss over how deep they actually were. There is a lingering anger, sometimes logical and sometimes illogical, as a result of this. And, having lived in South Africa for about twenty years, I find that I have internalised that anger because I have lived through enough experiences, subtle and overt, where I am judged by the colour of my skin, as opposed to the content of my character, to paraphrase Martin Luther King Jr. In those instances, all I can often do is simply be angry.

The cursed house

HE WAS adamant that our place had been cursed, cursed by my then girlfriend. The relationship was tumultuous enough as it was without these accusations of witchcraft. As to who the 'he' is, I'll leave that out. To maintain the semblance of peace, I suggested we visit a traditional healer (sangoma) I knew of in Soweto.

My father was a Christian growing up and, at the time he moved to Germany, he was a preacher of sorts. But, being in Europe in the late 1960s and early 1970s, he once mentioned in passing, seeing the plight of Africans and the Black man in Europe and across the world caused him to lose his faith.

Whatever the case was, although we lived in a predominantly Christian country, he allowed us, as children, to choose our own paths. Other than a brief stint in Scripture Union at the beginning of high school, and becoming 'born again' at a camp, I didn't then, or now, subscribe to any type of organised religion. I do, however, have a healthy respect for belief and people's chosen paths.

As a result of growing up in an accommodating environment, I have always drawn from different belief systems, including traditional African beliefs, which is what prompted my suggestion to my friend.

The sangoma, let's call him Baba Langa, is a fascinating man whose knowledge of African history and indigenous wisdom have been complemented by his travels and interactions with traditional healers from across the globe. The first consultation with him ended up running for hours because he had a captive audience to tell his stories to.

With regards to the cursing of the house, what he basically explained was that our ancestors serve as security of sorts and so, if you don't keep them updated on life stuff, there is no one to guard the gates of your spiritual garden. That, for me, was the end of that issue. I did, however, go back and see him twice more because of my own stuff.

When he threw the bones to ask my grandmother for permission to go through the process, it was an extended exercise because my African grandmother was Ghanaian while he is Zulu. He first had to explain that, while the ritual is different, the intention and purpose is to help her child, namely me. Once he had permission from her, he then, for lack of a better word, asked her to explain to my German grandmother that intention and get permission from her.

Once he was given permission, he could now deal with me directly. The summary is that, according to him, my mission in this physical realm is to serve as a bridge between cultures, considering I come from two different cultures and have been influenced by others. I was supposed to go back for further consultations but never got around to it; however, the idea of being a bridge has always stuck with me. It has taught me that life is not homogeneous and singular, and that empathy is a necessary trait if we want to live in harmony.

The broadness of my interests and influences has been helpful in this regard. The criteria I use are the diversity of my heritage and my interests. I try not to engage with life on the basis of the boxes or labels we, as human beings, are very good at trying to squeeze everything into but rather whether something resonates or not.

Keep going

THERE WAS a time when I willingly and comfortably wallowed in self-pity whenever it reared its head. Yes, the world was truly out to get me. Life was painful. Nothing ever went right, blah, blah, blah. I would drown my sorrows in many a bottle, drive a little faster, live a little more recklessly, and, even when those actions created more troubles, rinse and repeat. My father used to say it was all in the mind. I would laugh at him – internally – and veer down whatever destructive path lay before me.

It is a little uncomfortable to admit, to you and to myself, but I considered the perspective a tad foolish and a cop-out; looking at the things my father had to endure, it made no sense to me that he saw all of this as 'being in the mind'.

The beauty of life is that, if you open yourself up and listen, it will teach you the lessons along the way and, as I have morphed into a version of my father, or a better version of myself, built on the foundation of my father, it has started to make sense.

I once worked with someone who epitomised the expression 'bane of my existence' and, as a result, had such power over my days. I would wake up in the morning, full of life, looking forward to the day. I would get ready, drop the kids off at school and start my 30-minute drive to work. Without realising it, the closer I got to the office, the darker my mood would become. At least twice a week, by the time I parked my car, I could feel the start of a tension headache and, on days when that wasn't there, chances were high that by lunchtime I would have a full-blown headache.

This went on for two to three months. It had a real impact on how I felt physically, mentally and emotionally. I was coming home with that tension and it was impacting on how I related to my family. I was always stressed, always irritated, always on edge and always tired.

One day, I decided to approach it differently. I am not sure what sparked it. It may have been a song. It might have been a conversation with my father where he reiterated that it was all in the mind. It may have been the growing list of self-help-type books that I was reading. I know, in some spaces, there is a bit of a condescending attitude to self-help books, but I have found that, if you approach them with an open mind and don't get caught in the 'cultishness' of some of the personalities, there is always something to take away. Even if it is a single thought, I consider it worthwhile.

Anyway, the decision I took was that I was going to be happy when I got to work; I was not going to allow this one individual to determine how I felt and, as a result, how my life unfolded. It was giving him unbelievable power over me and my life.

There are many songs that make me feel good, whether in terms of the lyrics, the production or because they are just great to sing along to; songs like 'Optimistic' by Sounds of Blackness, 'Different Times' by Raphael Saadiq featuring T-Boz, Bruno Mars's 'Treasure' (which the Angel made me play every morning on the way to kindergarten for a good two months), 'Joints & Jam' by the Black Eyed Peas, 'Rock Steady' by The Whispers and The Gap Band's 'Outstanding'.

To reconfigure my mood every morning, I would choose a song and play that on repeat on my way into work, singing or rapping along, consciously getting myself into a great mood. And it worked. The headaches were gone. Walking into the office, my mood was upbeat. I had made the decision to be happy and I was, by and large, happier.

Since then, I have been very conscious and very deliberate about my state of mind and how that affects every aspect of my life. And I have become an it's-all-in-the-mind person. From John Kehoe's *Mind Power*, Paulo Coelho's *The Alchemist* and the writings of the Stoics (Marcus Aurelius, Epictetus and Seneca) to Robin Sharma's *The 5AM Club* and

Eckhart Tolle's *The Power of Now*, each one of these books, and many more, have contributed to changing the way I think about, look at and live life, internally.

There have been occasions when I have had to be the optimist, especially with my father and Gerrard, because it was very easy for us to all wallow in and be overwhelmed by the challenges that we were facing. I became the one focusing on the silver lining, always thinking positively. Since they both passed away, perhaps because I am in my head so much more and don't have them to allow me to step away for moments of respite, I find myself, on occasion, struggling to keep going.

At the height of the coronavirus lockdown, I was able to stay positive, despite the loss of work and income. I was able to stay – primarily – focused on things getting better. Yet, in a weird way, the shift to a more positive approach to life has made it harder to deal with the dips. And, sometimes, the dips happen daily. It is said that one should 'feel the feels' and allow oneself to not be okay, once in a while, and then get back up and move forward.

My fear is that, by doing so, I may end up back where I was: fatalistic, pessimistic and full of self-pity. It wasn't a nice place. This one is much nicer. I guess the only option is to keep going. To keep getting up every day believing that each day will be better.

Acknowledgements

THIS FEELS like writing an acceptance speech for an award I am yet to receive. How do I begin to acknowledge all the people who have had an impact on my life, however big or small, and helped me learn some of the lessons that are in this book? I would like to start off by thanking each and every person. As the saying goes, no man or woman is an island and I have been blessed enough to have so many come into my life. I appreciate you.

I am grateful to my family: my siblings, nephews and nieces, and extended, sometimes adopted family for the journey we have travelled thus far. It hasn't always been easy but, whether we like it or not, we are in this together. Although I may not always show it, I love you all very much.

A huge thank-you to Andrea Nattrass, Sibongile Machika and the team at Pan Macmillan for seeing merit in my telling my story. My writing a book has been a conversation Andrea and I have had for about eight years; I am glad that she continued to respond to my infrequent emails and that we finally found one that sticks. Thank you for guiding me through this process and dealing with my 'reflexive modesty' and self-doubt.

Thank you to Sally Hines for lending her eye to the pages and to my old friend, Victor Dlamini, for the photograph. It was supposed to be an author picture but what he made warranted a change in the cover design.

www.ingramcontent.com/pod-product-compliance
Lightning Source LLC
Chambersburg PA
CBHW020222170426
43201CB00007B/292